The Ultimate Guide to Digital Marketing: Bosot Your Online Presence and Drive Results

Margaret

Copyright © [2023]

Title: The Ultimate Guide to Digital Marketing: Bosot Your Online Presence and Drive Results
Author's: Margaret

All rights reserved. No part of this publication may be reproduced, stored in a retrieval system, or transmitted in any form or by any means, electronic, mechanical, photocopying, recording, or otherwise, without the prior written permission of the publisher or author, except in the case of brief quotations embodied in critical reviews and certain other non-commercial uses permitted by copyright law.

This book was printed and published by [Publisher's: **Margaret**] in [2023]

ISBN:

TABLE OF CONTENT

Chapter 1: Introduction to Digital Marketing   10

Understanding the Importance of Digital Marketing

Evolution of Digital Marketing

Benefits of Digital Marketing

Chapter 2: Search Engine Optimization (SEO)   17

Introduction to SEO

On-Page SEO Techniques

Off-Page SEO Techniques

Local SEO Strategies

SEO Analytics and Reporting

Chapter 3: Social Media Marketing   27

Introduction to Social Media Marketing

Creating a Social Media Strategy

Facebook Marketing Strategies

Instagram Marketing Strategies

Twitter Marketing Strategies

LinkedIn Marketing Strategies

Chapter 4: Email Marketing   40

Introduction to Email Marketing

Building an Email List

Crafting Effective Email Campaigns

Automation and Personalization in Email Marketing

Email Analytics and Optimization

Chapter 5: Content Marketing — 50

Introduction to Content Marketing

Developing a Content Marketing Strategy

Creating Engaging Blog Posts

Video Marketing Strategies

Infographic and Visual Content Marketing

Content Distribution and Promotion

Chapter 6: Conversion Rate Optimization — 62

Introduction to Conversion Rate Optimization (CRO)

Understanding User Experience (UX) Design

A/B Testing and Multivariate Testing

Landing Page Optimization

Call-to-Action (CTA) Optimization

Chapter 7: Analytics and Reporting 72

Introduction to Analytics and Reporting

Key Metrics in Digital Marketing

Using Google Analytics for Tracking and Analysis

Social Media Analytics and Insights

Reporting on ROI and Campaign Performance

Chapter 8: Mobile Marketing 83

Introduction to Mobile Marketing

Mobile Advertising Strategies

App Store Optimization (ASO)

Mobile-Friendly Website Design

SMS Marketing

Chapter 9: Influencer Marketing 93

Introduction to Influencer Marketing

Identifying and Collaborating with Influencers

Creating Effective Influencer Marketing Campaigns

Measuring the Success of Influencer Marketing

Chapter 10: E-commerce Marketing   101

Introduction to E-commerce Marketing

Setting up an Online Store

E-commerce SEO and SEM Strategies

Social Media Marketing for E-commerce

Retention Strategies for E-commerce

Chapter 11: Marketing Automation   111

Introduction to Marketing Automation

Implementing Marketing Automation Tools

Lead Generation and Nurturing with Marketing Automation

Personalization and Segmentation in Marketing Automation

Analyzing and Optimizing Marketing Automation Campaigns

Chapter 12: Emerging Trends in Digital Marketing   122

Artificial Intelligence (AI) in Digital Marketing

Voice Search and Digital Assistants

Augmented Reality (AR) and Virtual Reality (VR)

Chatbots and Conversational Marketing

Blockchain Technology and Cryptocurrency in Marketing

Chapter 13: Building a Successful Digital Marketing Career   132

Essential Skills for a Digital Marketer

Navigating the Job Market in Digital Marketing

Building a Personal Brand in the Digital Marketing Industry

Continuing Education and Professional Development

Success Stories and Inspiration from Digital Marketing Experts

Chapter 14: Conclusion 143

Recap of Key Concepts

Final Thoughts and Actionable Steps

Taking Your Digital Marketing Efforts to the Next Level

Chapter 1: Introduction to Digital Marketing

Understanding the Importance of Digital Marketing

In today's digital age, the success of any business, whether big or small, largely depends on its online presence. With the increasing use of technology and the internet, digital marketing has become an essential tool for businesses to reach their target audience and drive results. This subchapter aims to shed light on the importance of digital marketing in the context of digital business and how it can significantly impact your online success.

Digital marketing, simply put, refers to the use of digital channels and platforms such as websites, social media, search engines, email, and mobile applications to promote products and services. It allows businesses to connect with customers on a global scale, providing a level playing field for both established corporations and startups.

One of the key reasons why digital marketing is vital for digital businesses is its ability to reach a wider audience. Unlike traditional marketing methods, digital marketing allows you to target specific demographics, interests, and locations, ensuring that your message reaches the right people at the right time. With the vast amount of data available, you can analyze customer behavior and preferences, enabling you to tailor your marketing strategies and campaigns accordingly.

Moreover, digital marketing offers measurable results and analytics, giving you the opportunity to track your progress and make data-driven decisions. With tools like Google Analytics, you can monitor website traffic, conversion rates, and engagement levels, allowing you to refine your strategies and optimize your online presence.

Another significant advantage of digital marketing is its cost-effectiveness compared to traditional marketing methods. By utilizing digital platforms, businesses can reach a larger audience at a lower cost, making it a viable option for small businesses with limited marketing budgets.

Furthermore, digital marketing provides an avenue for building brand loyalty and customer engagement. Through social media platforms and email marketing, businesses can interact with their customers, address their concerns, and build lasting relationships. This direct communication fosters trust and credibility, ultimately leading to repeat business and customer advocacy.

In conclusion, understanding the importance of digital marketing is crucial for anyone involved in the digital business niche. Its ability to reach a wider audience, provide measurable results, and build customer engagement makes it an invaluable tool for boosting online presence and driving results. By harnessing the power of digital marketing, businesses can stay competitive in the digital landscape and thrive in today's fast-paced, technology-driven world.

Evolution of Digital Marketing

Introduction:
In this subchapter, we will explore the fascinating evolution of digital marketing and how it has transformed the way businesses reach and engage with their target audience. As technology continues to advance at an unprecedented rate, the strategies and techniques used in digital marketing have also undergone significant changes. Whether you are a seasoned digital marketer or just starting your digital business journey, understanding the evolution of this field is crucial to staying ahead in today's competitive landscape.

1. The Early Days:
Digital marketing traces its roots back to the early 1990s when the internet began to gain popularity. Websites were static, and businesses primarily relied on banner ads and email marketing to promote their products or services. While these methods were effective at the time, they lacked the personalization and targeting capabilities we enjoy today.

2. The Rise of Search Engines:
With the emergence of search engines like Yahoo and Google, digital marketing took a major leap forward. Marketers realized the potential of appearing at the top of search results and started optimizing their websites for better visibility. This gave birth to search engine optimization (SEO) and pay-per-click (PPC) advertising, which are still essential components of any digital marketing strategy.

3. Social Media Revolution:
The advent of social media platforms such as Facebook, Twitter, and

Instagram marked a significant turning point in digital marketing. Businesses could now engage with their target audience on a more personal level, building brand awareness and fostering customer loyalty. Social media marketing became a powerful tool for promoting products, sharing content, and running targeted ad campaigns.

4. Mobile Revolution:
The widespread adoption of smartphones revolutionized how people consume information and interact with brands. Mobile marketing became a necessity as businesses optimized their websites for mobile devices and created mobile apps to provide seamless user experiences. Location-based marketing and push notifications allowed for hyper-targeted advertising, further enhancing customer engagement.

5. The Age of Content Marketing:
As consumers became more discerning, businesses shifted their focus towards creating valuable and relevant content. Content marketing emerged as a key strategy, with blogs, videos, podcasts, and infographics used to educate and entertain audiences. This approach allowed companies to establish themselves as industry leaders while building trust and credibility with their customers.

Conclusion:
The evolution of digital marketing has been nothing short of extraordinary. From simple banner ads to sophisticated data-driven campaigns, businesses have had to adapt and innovate to keep pace with the changing digital landscape. As a digital business owner, staying informed about these advancements is paramount to achieving online success. By embracing the latest technologies and understanding consumer behavior, you can leverage the power of

digital marketing to boost your online presence, drive results, and stay ahead of the competition.

Benefits of Digital Marketing

In today's fast-paced digital world, digital marketing has become an essential tool for every business, regardless of its size or industry. The benefits of digital marketing are vast, and in this subchapter, we will explore how this powerful strategy can boost your online presence and drive remarkable results for your digital business.

One of the key advantages of digital marketing is its cost-effectiveness. Traditional marketing methods such as print ads or billboards can be quite expensive, making it difficult for small businesses to compete. However, with digital marketing, even businesses on a tight budget can reach their target audience through various cost-effective channels like social media, email marketing, or content marketing. This not only allows you to save money but also provides a higher return on investment compared to traditional marketing methods.

Another benefit of digital marketing is its ability to target specific demographics. Through advanced analytics and data tracking, digital marketers can identify their audience's preferences, interests, and behaviors. This valuable information enables businesses to create personalized and targeted campaigns, ensuring that their message reaches the right people at the right time. By understanding your audience better, you can tailor your marketing efforts to their needs, increasing the chances of conversion and customer loyalty.

Digital marketing also offers unparalleled flexibility and scalability. Unlike traditional marketing, which often requires lengthy planning and execution processes, digital marketing allows businesses to quickly adapt their strategies based on real-time data and market trends. You can easily modify your campaigns, experiment with different approaches, and measure their effectiveness in real-time. This agility not only saves time but also enables you to stay ahead of your competitors and respond to changes in the market swiftly.

Furthermore, digital marketing provides measurable results. Unlike traditional marketing methods, where it's challenging to determine the exact impact of your efforts, digital marketing provides comprehensive analytics and reporting tools. You can track the number of website visitors, conversion rates, engagement metrics, and other key performance indicators. By analyzing these metrics, you can gain valuable insights into the effectiveness of your campaigns and make data-driven decisions to optimize your marketing efforts.

Lastly, digital marketing opens up a world of global opportunities. With the internet connecting people around the globe, businesses can expand their reach beyond geographical boundaries. Whether you are a local business looking to attract customers from neighboring cities or a global brand aiming to reach an international audience, digital marketing provides the tools and platforms to connect with potential customers worldwide.

In conclusion, the benefits of digital marketing are undeniable for any digital business. From cost-effectiveness and targeted marketing to flexibility and global reach, digital marketing offers endless possibilities for driving online success. By embracing digital marketing strategies, businesses can boost their online presence, connect with their audience, and achieve remarkable results in today's digital age.

Chapter 2: Search Engine Optimization (SEO)

Introduction to SEO

In today's digital world, having a strong online presence is crucial for the success of any business. With more and more people turning to the internet to find products, services, and information, it's important for businesses to ensure that their websites are easily discoverable by potential customers. This is where Search Engine Optimization, or SEO, comes into play.

SEO is the practice of optimizing a website to improve its visibility on search engine results pages (SERPs). By utilizing various techniques and strategies, businesses can increase their organic, or non-paid, search engine rankings, ultimately driving more traffic to their websites. In this subchapter, we will delve into the fundamentals of SEO and how it can benefit your digital business.

First and foremost, it's essential to understand how search engines work. The most popular search engine, Google, uses complex algorithms to determine the relevance and quality of websites. These algorithms consider various factors such as keywords, website structure, user experience, and backlinks, among others. By understanding these factors, you can optimize your website to meet the requirements of search engines and improve your chances of ranking higher in the SERPs.

Keywords play a vital role in SEO. These are the words or phrases that users enter into search engines when looking for specific information. By conducting thorough keyword research, you can identify the most relevant and valuable keywords for your digital business. Incorporating these keywords into your website's content, meta tags, and URLs can significantly improve your search engine rankings.

Another crucial aspect of SEO is on-page optimization. This involves optimizing various elements on your website, such as title tags, meta descriptions, headings, and images. By ensuring that these elements are properly optimized with relevant keywords, search engines can better understand the content of your website, leading to improved visibility in search results.

Off-page optimization is equally important in SEO. This refers to activities that take place outside of your website, such as link building and social media marketing. Building high-quality backlinks from reputable websites can boost your website's credibility and authority in the eyes of search engines, leading to higher rankings.

In conclusion, SEO is a fundamental aspect of digital marketing that can significantly impact the success of your online business. By optimizing your website for search engines, you can increase your visibility, drive more organic traffic, and ultimately achieve better results. In the following chapters, we will delve deeper into the various strategies and techniques that can help you master the art of SEO and take your digital business to new heights.

On-Page SEO Techniques

In today's digital business landscape, having a strong online presence is crucial for success. One of the most effective ways to boost your online visibility and drive results is through implementing On-Page SEO techniques. By optimizing the content and structure of your website, you can improve your search engine rankings and attract more organic traffic. In this subchapter, we will explore the essential On-Page SEO techniques that can help you achieve these goals.

First and foremost, it is important to conduct thorough keyword research. By identifying the keywords and phrases that your target audience is using to search for products or services similar to yours, you can strategically incorporate them into your website's content. This will enable search engines to understand the relevance of your website and rank it higher in search results.

Next, focus on creating high-quality, engaging, and relevant content. Search engines prioritize websites that provide valuable information to users. By producing regular blog posts, articles, and other forms of content that answer your audience's questions, you can establish yourself as an authority in your niche and improve your search engine rankings.

Another important On-Page SEO technique is optimizing your website's meta tags. These include the title tag, meta description, and header tags. By using descriptive and keyword-rich tags, you can not only improve your website's visibility in search results but also entice users to click on your website.

Additionally, pay attention to your website's URL structure. A well-structured URL that includes relevant keywords helps search engines understand the content of your page and improves its chances of ranking higher. Make sure to use hyphens to separate words in your URL and keep it concise and descriptive.

Lastly, optimize your website's images and videos. Use descriptive file names and alt tags to make it easier for search engines to index and understand your media content. Compress your images to reduce loading time, as slow-loading pages can negatively impact your search engine rankings.

In conclusion, On-Page SEO techniques are vital for any digital business striving to boost its online presence and drive results. By conducting comprehensive keyword research, creating valuable content, optimizing meta tags and URL structure, and optimizing multimedia content, you can improve your website's visibility, attract more organic traffic, and ultimately achieve your online marketing goals. Implement these techniques consistently, and you will witness a significant improvement in your search engine rankings and overall online performance.

Off-Page SEO Techniques

In the ever-evolving digital landscape, having a strong online presence is crucial for any business. And when it comes to digital business, search engine optimization (SEO) plays a vital role in driving organic traffic and boosting website rankings. While on-page SEO focuses on optimizing website elements, off-page SEO techniques are equally important to enhance your online visibility and authority. In this subchapter, we will delve into the world of off-page SEO techniques and explore the strategies that can elevate your digital business to new heights.

Off-page SEO primarily involves activities that take place outside your website but have a significant impact on its search engine rankings. The most prominent off-page SEO technique is link building. By acquiring high-quality backlinks from reputable websites, search engines perceive your website as trustworthy and authoritative. We will discuss various link building strategies, such as guest blogging, influencer outreach, and social bookmarking, to empower you to build a robust network of backlinks.

Another crucial off-page SEO technique is social media marketing. With billions of people engaging on social media platforms, leveraging these channels can drive immense traffic to your website. We will explore effective social media marketing strategies, including content optimization, community engagement, and influencer collaborations, to help you harness the power of social media for your digital business.

Additionally, we will discuss the importance of online reputation management (ORM). In the digital era, your online reputation can make or break your business. We will provide insights on how to monitor and manage your online reputation effectively, including tips for handling negative reviews and leveraging positive customer feedback to enhance your brand image.

Furthermore, we will touch upon the significance of content marketing in off-page SEO. Creating valuable, shareable content not only attracts visitors but also encourages others to link back to your website. We will provide practical tips and strategies to help you create compelling content that resonates with your target audience and drives engagement.

In conclusion, off-page SEO techniques are essential for any digital business looking to boost its online presence and drive results. By implementing effective link building strategies, leveraging social media marketing, managing your online reputation, and investing in content marketing, you can significantly enhance your website's visibility, authority, and organic traffic. Stay tuned as we explore each of these techniques in detail and equip you with the tools and knowledge to succeed in the digital marketing landscape.

Local SEO Strategies

In today's digital world, having a strong online presence is crucial for any business, especially those operating in the digital business niche. One of the most effective ways to boost your online visibility and drive results is through local SEO strategies. Local SEO focuses on optimizing your website and online content to attract local customers and improve your search engine rankings in specific geographic areas.

First and foremost, it is essential to ensure that your website is optimized for local searches. This includes adding your business's name, address, and phone number (NAP) to each page of your website. Additionally, creating specific landing pages for each location you serve can significantly enhance your local SEO efforts. These landing pages should contain relevant keywords, unique content, and a clear call-to-action to encourage potential customers to take action.

Another vital aspect of local SEO is optimizing your Google My Business (GMB) listing. GMB is a free tool provided by Google that allows businesses to manage their online presence, including their appearance in Google Maps and local search results. To make the most of your GMB listing, ensure that all your business information is accurate and up-to-date. Encourage customers to leave positive reviews, as these can significantly impact your local search rankings.

Consistency is key when it comes to local SEO. Make sure your business information is consistent across all online platforms, including your website, social media profiles, and online directories. This includes your business name, address, phone number, and even your website URL. Inconsistencies can confuse search engines and potential customers, leading to lower rankings and fewer conversions.

Additionally, taking advantage of local keywords and creating locally-focused content is essential for improving your local search rankings. Conduct keyword research to identify relevant keywords that potential customers in your area are using to find businesses like yours. Incorporate these keywords naturally into your website content, blog posts, and social media updates to increase your chances of being found by local searchers.

Furthermore, leveraging online business directories and local citation opportunities can significantly boost your local SEO efforts. Submitting your business information to reputable directories such as Yelp, Yellow Pages, and Bing Places can help improve your online visibility and credibility. Additionally, getting listed on local directories specific to your area or industry can further enhance your local search rankings.

In conclusion, local SEO strategies are crucial for any business operating in the digital business niche. By optimizing your website, leveraging GMB, ensuring consistency across online platforms, targeting local keywords, and utilizing online directories, you can greatly improve your online presence and drive results. Implementing these local SEO techniques will help you attract more local customers, increase your search engine rankings, and ultimately drive more traffic and revenue for your business.

SEO Analytics and Reporting

In today's digital business landscape, it is crucial to have a strong online presence to drive results and stay ahead of the competition. Search Engine Optimization (SEO) plays a vital role in improving your website's visibility and driving organic traffic. However, implementing SEO strategies is not enough; you need to measure and analyze their effectiveness to continuously improve your online presence. This is where SEO analytics and reporting come into play.

SEO analytics refers to the process of collecting and analyzing data related to your website's performance on search engines. It involves tracking various metrics like organic traffic, keyword rankings, click-through rates, bounce rates, and conversion rates. By analyzing these metrics, you can gain valuable insights into how well your website is performing and identify areas for improvement.

One of the most widely used tools for SEO analytics is Google Analytics. It provides comprehensive data on your website's traffic, user behavior, and conversions. By setting up goals and funnels, you can track the performance of specific pages or actions on your website. Google Search Console is another valuable tool that helps you monitor your website's performance in search results, identify crawl errors, and improve your site's visibility.

Reporting is an integral part of SEO analytics as it helps you communicate your website's performance to stakeholders effectively. Regular reporting allows you to showcase the impact of your SEO efforts and justify your investment. It also helps you track progress over time and identify trends or patterns that can inform your future strategies.

When creating SEO reports, it's important to focus on key performance indicators (KPIs) that align with your business objectives. Some common KPIs include organic traffic growth, keyword rankings, conversion rates, and revenue generated from organic search. Visualizing data through charts, graphs, and tables can make your reports more engaging and easier to understand.

By regularly analyzing SEO data and creating insightful reports, you can make data-driven decisions to optimize your website's performance. Whether you are a digital business owner, marketing professional, or anyone interested in boosting their online presence, understanding SEO analytics and reporting is essential for success in the digital realm.

In conclusion, SEO analytics and reporting are vital components of any digital business strategy. By leveraging tools like Google Analytics and Search Console, you can gain valuable insights into your website's performance and continuously improve your online presence. Regular reporting helps you communicate the impact of your SEO efforts and make data-driven decisions to drive results. So, start harnessing the power of SEO analytics and reporting to boost your online presence and achieve your business goals.

Chapter 3: Social Media Marketing

Introduction to Social Media Marketing

Social media has revolutionized the way businesses connect with their customers and promote their products or services. In today's digital business landscape, it has become essential for every business, regardless of its size or industry, to have a strong presence on social media platforms. This subchapter aims to provide an introduction to social media marketing, exploring its significance and how it can help boost your online presence and drive results.

Social media marketing is the process of utilizing various social media platforms to engage with a target audience, build brand awareness, and drive traffic to a website or online store. With billions of active users worldwide, platforms like Facebook, Instagram, Twitter, LinkedIn, and YouTube offer unprecedented opportunities for businesses to reach a vast audience and establish meaningful connections.

One of the key advantages of social media marketing is its cost-effectiveness. Unlike traditional advertising methods, such as television or print ads, social media allows businesses to promote their products or services at a fraction of the cost. This makes it particularly appealing for digital businesses with limited marketing budgets.

Additionally, social media marketing provides businesses with the ability to target specific demographics and interests. Through advanced targeting options, businesses can ensure their content reaches the right audience, increasing the likelihood of conversion and customer engagement.

Moreover, social media platforms offer a variety of tools and features that can help businesses measure the effectiveness of their marketing efforts. From analytics to track engagement and reach to conversion tracking, these tools provide valuable insights into the success of your social media campaigns and allow you to make data-driven decisions.

However, it is important to note that social media marketing is not a one-size-fits-all approach. Every social media platform has its own unique characteristics, user demographics, and best practices. It is crucial for digital businesses to understand their target audience and select the platforms that align with their goals and objectives.

In this subchapter, we will delve deeper into the world of social media marketing, exploring strategies, tips, and best practices to help you navigate the ever-changing social media landscape. From creating compelling content to engaging with your audience and measuring your results, this subchapter will equip you with the knowledge and tools necessary to boost your online presence and drive tangible results through social media marketing.

Creating a Social Media Strategy

In today's digital age, social media has become an integral part of our lives. It has revolutionized the way businesses connect with their audience and market their products or services. To harness the power of social media and boost your online presence, it is essential to have a well-defined social media strategy. This subchapter will guide you through the process of creating an effective social media strategy that will drive results for your digital business.

First and foremost, it is crucial to identify your goals and objectives. What do you want to achieve through social media? Is it to increase brand awareness, generate leads, drive website traffic, or engage with your audience? Clearly defining your goals will help you develop a focused strategy tailored to your specific needs.

Next, conduct thorough research to understand your target audience. Who are they? What platforms do they use? What content do they engage with? By understanding your audience's preferences and behavior, you can create content that resonates with them and maximize your impact.

Choose the right social media platforms that align with your target audience and business goals. Each platform has its unique features and audience demographics. For instance, if you are targeting a younger audience, platforms like Instagram and TikTok may be more suitable, whereas LinkedIn might be ideal for B2B businesses. It is essential to evaluate which platforms will yield the best results for your business.

Once you've selected your platforms, develop a content strategy. Consistency is key when it comes to social media. Plan and create engaging and informative content that aligns with your brand's voice and values. Utilize a mix of text, images, videos, and infographics to keep your content varied and appealing. Don't forget to incorporate relevant hashtags and keywords to improve discoverability.

Engagement is the backbone of social media success. Interact with your audience by responding to comments, messages, and mentions. Encourage conversations, ask questions, and seek feedback. Building genuine relationships with your followers will enhance brand loyalty and drive word-of-mouth marketing.

Lastly, measure your social media efforts using analytics tools. Track key metrics such as reach, engagement, conversions, and website traffic. Analyzing this data will provide valuable insights into what's working and what needs improvement, enabling you to refine your strategy for better results.

In conclusion, a well-crafted social media strategy is essential for any digital business looking to boost their online presence. By setting clear goals, understanding your audience, choosing the right platforms, creating engaging content, fostering engagement, and measuring results, you can develop a successful social media strategy that drives tangible outcomes for your business. Embrace the power of social media and unlock its full potential to thrive in the digital landscape.

Facebook Marketing Strategies

In this subchapter, we will dive into the realm of Facebook marketing strategies, exploring the various ways in which businesses can leverage this powerful social media platform to boost their online presence and drive tangible results. Whether you are an entrepreneur, a small business owner, or a digital marketing enthusiast, this section will equip you with the knowledge and tools needed to effectively utilize Facebook for your digital business.

1. Establishing a Facebook Business Page: The first step towards successful Facebook marketing is creating a professional and engaging business page. We will guide you through the process of setting up your page, optimizing it for search engines, and incorporating compelling visuals and content to capture the attention of your target audience.

2. Defining Your Target Audience: Identifying your target audience is crucial for creating relevant and engaging content. We will discuss strategies for understanding your audience's demographics, interests, and online behavior, enabling you to tailor your Facebook marketing efforts to effectively connect with them.

3. Content Creation and Curation: Facebook is all about content, and we will teach you how to create and curate compelling content that resonates with your audience. From engaging posts, videos, and images to interactive live sessions and stories, we will explore the various content formats that can help you captivate and retain your Facebook followers.

4. Paid Advertising on Facebook: Facebook's advertising platform offers a plethora of targeting options and ad formats to reach your desired audience. We will delve into the world of Facebook ads, discussing strategies for choosing the right ad campaign objectives, targeting options, and ad formats to maximize your return on investment.

5. Engaging Your Audience: Building a loyal and engaged community on Facebook is key to long-term success. We will provide you with strategies for fostering meaningful interactions, responding to comments and messages, and leveraging Facebook groups and events to create a sense of community around your brand.

6. Measuring and Analyzing Results: To ensure your Facebook marketing efforts are driving results, you need to measure and analyze the outcomes. We will introduce you to Facebook Insights and other analytics tools, enabling you to track key performance indicators and make data-driven decisions to optimize your Facebook marketing strategy.

By implementing the strategies outlined in this subchapter, you will be well-equipped to harness the power of Facebook to boost your online presence, engage with your target audience, and drive tangible results for your digital business. Whether you are a novice or experienced marketer, these proven Facebook marketing strategies will empower you to stay ahead in the ever-evolving world of digital marketing.

Instagram Marketing Strategies

In the fast-paced world of digital business, establishing a strong online presence is crucial for success. One platform that has revolutionized the way businesses connect with their audience is Instagram. With its massive user base of over one billion active users, Instagram presents a unique opportunity for businesses to enhance their brand visibility and drive results. In this subchapter, we will explore some effective Instagram marketing strategies that can help you boost your online presence and achieve your business goals.

1. Define Your Goals: Before diving into Instagram marketing, it is essential to establish clear goals. Whether you aim to increase brand awareness, drive website traffic, or generate leads, having a specific objective will guide your strategy and enable you to measure success.

2. Optimize Your Profile: Your Instagram profile is a reflection of your brand. Ensure that your username, bio, and profile picture accurately represent your business. Use relevant keywords and hashtags in your bio to improve discoverability.

3. Engaging Content Strategy: Instagram is a visual platform, so focus on creating high-quality and visually appealing content. Experiment with different formats like photos, videos, and stories to keep your audience engaged. Use a mix of curated content, user-generated content, and behind-the-scenes glimpses to showcase your brand's personality.

4. Hashtag Research: Hashtags are a powerful tool for increasing your reach and engagement on Instagram. Research popular and industry-specific hashtags related to your content and incorporate them

strategically in your posts. Aim for a mix of broad and niche hashtags to target a wider audience.

5. Consistent Posting Schedule: To stay top-of-mind with your audience, maintain a consistent posting schedule. Post at optimal times when your target audience is most active on the platform. Use Instagram Insights to analyze your audience's behavior and identify the best times to reach them.

6. Engage with Your Audience: Instagram is all about building connections. Respond to comments, direct messages, and mentions promptly. Show appreciation for your followers by liking and commenting on their posts. Encourage user-generated content by running contests or featuring customer testimonials.

7. Collaborations and Influencer Marketing: Partnering with influencers or relevant businesses can amplify your brand's reach. Identify influencers in your niche and collaborate with them to create sponsored content or host giveaways. This can expose your brand to a new audience and boost your credibility.

8. Instagram Ads: Utilize Instagram's advertising platform to reach a wider audience and achieve specific objectives. Experiment with different ad formats like photo ads, video ads, and carousel ads to see what resonates best with your target audience.

By implementing these Instagram marketing strategies, you can leverage the power of this popular platform to boost your online presence, connect with your audience, and drive tangible results for your digital business. Remember to continuously analyze your efforts, adapt your strategy, and stay up-to-date with the latest trends and features to maximize your success on Instagram.

Twitter Marketing Strategies

In today's digital business landscape, having a strong online presence is crucial for success. One platform that stands out for its ability to connect businesses with their target audience and drive results is Twitter. With over 330 million monthly active users, Twitter offers a unique opportunity for businesses to engage with their customers, build brand awareness, and drive traffic to their websites. In this subchapter, we will explore effective Twitter marketing strategies that can help you boost your online presence and drive meaningful results.

1. Define Your Objectives: Before diving into Twitter marketing, it's essential to identify your goals. Are you looking to increase brand awareness, generate leads, drive website traffic, or engage with your customers? Defining your objectives will help you tailor your Twitter marketing strategies accordingly.

2. Optimize Your Profile: Your Twitter profile serves as the first impression for potential customers. Ensure that your profile picture, header image, and bio accurately represent your brand. Use keywords relevant to your niche in your bio to make it easier for users to find you.

3. Create Engaging Content: To capture the attention of your audience, focus on creating valuable and engaging content. Share industry news, tips, and insights that resonate with your target audience. Incorporate visuals such as images and videos to make your tweets more appealing.

4. Use Hashtags Strategically: Hashtags play a significant role in Twitter marketing by making your content discoverable to a wider

audience. Research popular hashtags relevant to your industry and incorporate them into your tweets. Additionally, create your branded hashtag to encourage user-generated content and increase brand visibility.

5. Engage with Your Audience: Twitter is a social platform, so it's essential to engage with your followers. Respond to their comments, retweet their content, and participate in relevant conversations. Building relationships with your audience can lead to increased brand loyalty and advocacy.

6. Utilize Twitter Ads: Twitter offers various advertising options to help businesses reach their target audience effectively. Experiment with promoted tweets, accounts, and trends to increase your visibility and reach a broader audience. Set clear objectives, target the right audience, and monitor your ad performance to optimize your campaigns.

7. Analyze and Adapt: Regularly monitor your Twitter analytics to gain insights into what strategies are working and what needs improvement. Analyze metrics such as engagement rate, reach, and click-through rates to refine your Twitter marketing strategies continually.

Twitter can be a powerful tool for digital business owners to connect with their audience and drive results. By implementing these Twitter marketing strategies, you can boost your online presence, increase brand awareness, and ultimately drive meaningful results for your business.

LinkedIn Marketing Strategies

LinkedIn has emerged as one of the most powerful platforms for digital marketing in recent years. With its vast network of professionals and businesses, it offers immense opportunities to boost your online presence and drive results. In this subchapter, we will explore a range of LinkedIn marketing strategies that can help you effectively promote your digital business.

1. Create a compelling company page: Your company page on LinkedIn acts as a virtual storefront, providing potential customers with valuable information about your brand. Ensure that your page is visually appealing, includes a concise yet impactful description, and highlights key offerings and achievements.

2. Optimize your profile: Your personal LinkedIn profile is equally important. Optimize it by using relevant keywords, showcasing your expertise, and including links to your website and other social media profiles. This will enhance your visibility and credibility among your target audience.

3. Publish engaging content: LinkedIn's publishing platform allows you to share informative articles, industry insights, and thought leadership pieces. Develop a content strategy that aligns with your digital business niche and consistently publish high-quality content to establish yourself as an authority in your field.

4. Engage in groups and communities: Join relevant LinkedIn groups and communities to connect with like-minded professionals and potential customers. Engage in discussions, share valuable insights,

and provide solutions to establish yourself as a knowledgeable and trustworthy expert.

5. Leverage LinkedIn advertising: LinkedIn's advertising features enable you to target specific demographics, industries, and job titles. Create compelling ads that resonate with your target audience and drive them towards your website or landing pages.

6. Utilize LinkedIn Pulse: LinkedIn Pulse is a powerful tool for distributing your content to a broader audience. Repurpose your blog posts or articles to reach a wider network, and encourage engagement through likes, comments, and shares.

7. Build strategic partnerships: LinkedIn enables you to connect with industry influencers, potential collaborators, and complementary businesses. Leverage these connections to create mutually beneficial partnerships that can expand your reach and attract new customers.

8. Monitor analytics and adapt: LinkedIn provides comprehensive analytics that track the performance of your posts, ads, and overall engagement. Regularly review these metrics to identify what works best for your digital business and make necessary adjustments to optimize your marketing strategies.

By implementing these LinkedIn marketing strategies, you can effectively boost your online presence, expand your network, and drive tangible results for your digital business. Stay proactive, consistent, and adaptable, and you will reap the benefits of LinkedIn's immense marketing potential.

Chapter 4: Email Marketing

Introduction to Email Marketing

Email marketing is a powerful tool that has revolutionized the way businesses communicate with their customers. In today's digital age, where everyone is connected through various devices, email remains a reliable and effective method of reaching a wide audience. Whether you are a small business owner, an entrepreneur, or a digital marketer, understanding the basics of email marketing is essential to boost your online presence and drive results.

This chapter will serve as an introduction to email marketing, covering the fundamentals and providing you with insights on how to leverage this strategy for your digital business. We will explore the various aspects of email marketing, including its benefits, strategies, and best practices.

First and foremost, let's understand why email marketing is crucial for any digital business. It is a cost-effective way to reach a large number of potential customers instantly. Unlike other marketing channels, emails provide a personalized touch and allow you to tailor your message to specific target audiences. Furthermore, email marketing enables you to build long-term relationships with your subscribers, nurturing them into loyal customers.

To effectively implement email marketing, you need to understand the key strategies involved. We will discuss the importance of building an email list and how to grow it organically. You will learn about the different types of emails you can send, such as newsletters, promotional emails, and automated drip campaigns. We will also delve into the importance of creating compelling and engaging email content that resonates with your audience.

In addition to strategies, we will explore the best practices that can maximize the effectiveness of your email marketing campaigns. You will discover the importance of segmenting your email list, personalizing your messages, and optimizing for mobile devices. We will also cover email deliverability and how to avoid spam filters, ensuring that your emails reach the intended recipients.

By the end of this chapter, you will have a solid understanding of email marketing and its potential to boost your online presence. Whether you are just starting or looking to enhance your existing email marketing efforts, the insights shared here will equip you with the necessary knowledge to drive results for your digital business. So, let's dive in and explore the world of email marketing together!

Building an Email List

In today's digital business landscape, one of the most valuable assets you can have is a strong and engaged email list. An email list is a compilation of email addresses that have been willingly provided by individuals who are interested in your products or services. This list allows you to directly reach out to your audience, share valuable content, and ultimately drive results for your digital business.

Why is building an email list so important? Well, unlike other digital marketing strategies that rely on algorithms or changing platforms, an email list is something you own. It is a direct line of communication with your audience that cannot be taken away or manipulated by external factors. With email marketing, you are in control of the message, the timing, and the targeting.

So, how can you build an email list that is not only substantial in size but also filled with engaged subscribers? Here are some effective strategies to consider:

1. Create valuable lead magnets: Offer free resources, such as e-books, checklists, or templates, in exchange for email addresses. These lead magnets should provide real value to your audience and address their pain points.

2. Optimize your website for conversions: Place prominent opt-in forms on your website, such as pop-ups, slide-ins, or inline forms. Make sure they are visually appealing and offer a clear benefit for subscribing.

3. Use social media to your advantage: Promote your lead magnets and encourage followers to join your email list. Leverage the power of social media platforms by running targeted ad campaigns to reach your ideal audience.

4. Host webinars or online events: Offer valuable content through live webinars or virtual events, and require attendees to register with their email addresses. This not only helps you grow your list but also positions you as an authority in your niche.

5. Offer exclusive discounts or promotions: Provide special offers or discounts exclusively to your email subscribers. This creates a sense of exclusivity and incentivizes people to join your list.

Remember, building an email list is an ongoing process. It requires consistent effort, creativity, and a focus on providing value to your audience. As your list grows, make sure to segment your subscribers based on their interests and preferences, allowing you to deliver personalized and targeted content.

In conclusion, building an email list is a crucial aspect of any successful digital business. It provides a direct line of communication with your audience, allowing you to nurture relationships, drive conversions, and ultimately boost your online presence. Implement these strategies and watch your email list grow, bringing you closer to achieving your digital marketing goals.

Crafting Effective Email Campaigns

In today's digital business landscape, email marketing remains one of the most powerful tools to engage with your audience and drive results. Whether you are a seasoned marketer or just starting out, understanding how to craft effective email campaigns can make a significant difference in your online presence. This subchapter of "The Ultimate Guide to Digital Marketing" delves into the strategies and best practices for creating email campaigns that captivate your audience and deliver measurable results.

Effective email campaigns start with a clear and compelling message. They are carefully crafted to resonate with the target audience and provide value. It is essential to understand your audience's pain points, desires, and interests to create content that speaks directly to them. By segmenting your email list based on demographics, preferences, or past interactions, you can personalize your campaigns and send targeted messages that are more likely to resonate.

Another crucial aspect of crafting effective email campaigns is to optimize the design and layout. Emails should be visually appealing, easy to read, and reflect your brand's identity. Use eye-catching subject lines to capture attention, and keep the email copy concise and engaging. Visual elements, such as images or infographics, can enhance the reader's experience and convey information effectively.

Furthermore, effective email campaigns rely on a strong call-to-action (CTA). Whether you want your readers to make a purchase, sign up for a webinar, or download an e-book, your CTA should be clear, persuasive, and strategically placed. The language used in the CTA should be action-oriented and encourage immediate response.

Additionally, it is crucial to track and analyze the performance of your email campaigns. Use data analytics tools to measure open rates, click-through rates, and conversions. A thorough analysis of this data will provide insights into what resonates with your audience and enable you to refine your future campaigns for better results.

In conclusion, crafting effective email campaigns is an essential skill for digital businesses of all sizes. By understanding your audience, optimizing design, creating compelling content, and using strong CTAs, you can engage with your subscribers and drive measurable results. Remember to continuously analyze your campaigns' performance and adapt your strategies accordingly. With the knowledge gained from this subchapter, you will be well-equipped to harness the power of email marketing and boost your online presence.

Automation and Personalization in Email Marketing

In today's fast-paced digital business landscape, email marketing continues to be a powerful tool for connecting with customers, driving sales, and boosting brand awareness. However, the key to success lies in effectively utilizing automation and personalization strategies. This subchapter explores the importance of automation and personalization in email marketing and how it can help businesses thrive in the digital world.

Automation is the process of using software and tools to automate repetitive tasks, such as sending out emails, tracking customer behavior, and analyzing data. By automating email marketing campaigns, businesses can save time, increase efficiency, and ensure consistent communication with their audience. Automation allows marketers to set up triggers and workflows that send personalized emails based on specific actions or behaviors, such as abandoned shopping carts, previous purchases, or website visits. This level of automation enables businesses to engage with their customers at the right time with the right content, ultimately increasing conversions and customer loyalty.

Personalization, on the other hand, involves tailoring emails to individual recipients based on their preferences, interests, and previous interactions. With advancements in technology and data analytics, businesses can now gather valuable information about their customers, such as demographics, purchase history, and browsing habits. Armed with this data, marketers can create highly targeted and personalized email campaigns that resonate with each recipient, offering relevant content and recommendations. Personalization not only helps businesses stand out in crowded inboxes but also strengthens customer relationships by showing that they are valued and understood.

By combining automation and personalization in email marketing, businesses can achieve remarkable results. Automated personalized emails have been proven to drive higher open rates, click-through rates, and conversions compared to generic mass emails. Moreover, the ability to segment and target specific customer groups allows businesses to deliver more relevant content, leading to improved customer satisfaction and increased brand loyalty.

In conclusion, automation and personalization are vital components of successful email marketing campaigns in the digital business era. By harnessing the power of automation, businesses can streamline their email marketing efforts, save time, and boost efficiency. Personalization, on the other hand, enables businesses to connect with customers on a deeper level by delivering tailored content and recommendations. By leveraging these strategies, businesses can maximize the impact of their email marketing campaigns, driving results and strengthening their online presence.

Email Analytics and Optimization

In today's digital business landscape, email marketing has become a vital tool for businesses of all sizes. It allows companies to directly connect with their audience, build relationships, and drive conversions. However, simply sending out emails is not enough. To truly harness the power of email marketing, businesses must dive into email analytics and optimization.

Email analytics provides valuable insights into the effectiveness of your email campaigns. It allows you to track and measure various metrics, such as open rates, click-through rates, and conversion rates. By analyzing these metrics, you can gain a deeper understanding of your audience's behavior and preferences. This knowledge enables you to make data-driven decisions and optimize your email marketing strategy for maximum impact.

One of the key metrics to focus on is the open rate. This metric indicates how many recipients actually opened your email. A low open rate may suggest that your subject lines are not compelling enough or that your emails are being marked as spam. By testing different subject lines and analyzing the open rates, you can identify what resonates with your audience and improve your email open rates.

Another important metric is the click-through rate (CTR) which tells you how many recipients clicked on a link within your email. A high CTR indicates that your content is engaging and relevant. To optimize your CTR, consider personalizing your emails and segmenting your audience based on their interests and preferences. This way, you can send targeted emails that are tailored to each recipient's needs, increasing the likelihood of them clicking through.

Conversion rate is another critical metric to monitor. It measures the percentage of recipients who take the desired action, such as making a purchase or signing up for a webinar. To optimize your conversion rate, ensure your email content is persuasive, visually appealing, and includes a clear call-to-action. Experiment with different designs, layouts, and CTAs to find what resonates best with your audience.

Email analytics also allows you to track metrics such as bounce rate, unsubscribe rate, and spam complaints. These metrics provide valuable insights into the quality of your email list and the relevance of your content. By monitoring and optimizing these metrics, you can ensure your email campaigns are reaching the right audience and delivering value.

In conclusion, email analytics and optimization are essential for any digital business looking to enhance their email marketing efforts. By analyzing key metrics and making data-driven decisions, you can continuously optimize your email campaigns to drive better results. Remember to test and experiment with different strategies, and always keep your audience's preferences and behaviors in mind. With the right approach, email marketing can become a powerful tool for boosting your online presence and driving conversions.

Chapter 5: Content Marketing

Introduction to Content Marketing

In today's digital business landscape, having a strong online presence is crucial for success. Whether you are a small business owner, an entrepreneur, or a marketing professional, understanding the power of content marketing is essential to boost your online presence and drive results. This subchapter will serve as your comprehensive guide to the world of content marketing, providing you with the knowledge and tools to leverage this powerful strategy effectively.

Content marketing is the art of creating and distributing valuable, relevant, and consistent content to attract and engage a specific audience. Unlike traditional advertising, content marketing focuses on building trust and establishing a long-term relationship with your target audience. By providing valuable information, insights, and solutions, you position yourself as an authority in your niche and gain the loyalty and trust of your customers.

In this digital age, consumers have become more discerning and selective about the content they consume. They seek relevant and engaging information that adds value to their lives. This is where content marketing comes into play. By delivering high-quality, informative, and entertaining content, you can capture the attention of your target audience and keep them coming back for more.

This subchapter will delve into the various aspects of content marketing, including the importance of developing a content strategy, understanding your target audience, creating compelling content, and distributing it through the appropriate channels. We will explore different content formats, such as blog posts, videos, podcasts, infographics, and social media posts, and discuss how to optimize them for maximum engagement.

Additionally, we will discuss the role of SEO (Search Engine Optimization) in content marketing, as well as the importance of analytics and measurement in evaluating the success of your content marketing efforts. You will learn how to track and analyze key metrics to fine-tune your content strategy and ensure that your efforts are driving the desired results.

By the end of this subchapter, you will have a solid understanding of the fundamentals of content marketing and how it can benefit your digital business. Armed with this knowledge, you will be able to create a robust content marketing strategy that effectively attracts, engages, and converts your target audience, ultimately boosting your online presence and driving tangible results.

Developing a Content Marketing Strategy

In today's digital landscape, content marketing has become a vital tool for businesses to boost their online presence and drive results. Whether you are a small startup or a well-established organization, having a well-defined content marketing strategy can help you connect with your target audience, establish credibility, and ultimately drive conversions. This subchapter will guide you through the process of developing an effective content marketing strategy that aligns with your digital business goals.

Understanding Your Audience: The first step in developing a content marketing strategy is to understand your target audience. Who are they? What are their pain points, needs, and desires? By conducting thorough market research, you can gain valuable insights into your audience's demographics, behaviors, and preferences. This knowledge will enable you to create content that resonates with them and addresses their specific needs.

Defining Your Goals: Once you have a clear understanding of your audience, it's essential to define your goals. What do you want to achieve through content marketing? Are you looking to increase brand awareness, drive website traffic, generate leads, or boost sales? Setting specific and measurable goals will help you focus your efforts and track your progress effectively.

Creating Engaging Content: The heart of any content marketing strategy lies in creating high-quality and engaging content. This content can take various forms, including blog posts, videos, podcasts, infographics, and social media posts. The key is to provide valuable information, entertain, inspire, or educate your audience. Your content should be well-researched, authentic, and aligned with your brand's voice and values.

Selecting Distribution Channels: Once you have created compelling content, it's time to decide on the most effective distribution channels. Consider where your target audience spends their time online and choose platforms that allow you to reach them directly. This may include social media channels, email marketing, influencer partnerships, or even guest blogging on industry-related websites.

Measuring and Analyzing: To ensure the success of your content marketing strategy, it's crucial to measure and analyze its performance regularly. Utilize analytics tools to track key metrics such as website traffic, engagement rates, conversions, and social media reach. This data will provide valuable insights into what's working and what can be improved, allowing you to make data-driven decisions and refine your strategy.

In conclusion, developing a content marketing strategy is essential for any digital business looking to thrive in today's competitive landscape. By understanding your audience, setting clear goals, creating engaging content, selecting the right distribution channels, and measuring your results, you can effectively boost your online presence and drive the desired outcomes. Remember, a well-executed content marketing strategy can be a game-changer for your business, helping you stand out, build meaningful connections, and achieve long-term success.

Creating Engaging Blog Posts

In today's digital business landscape, having a strong online presence is crucial for success. One of the most effective ways to boost your online presence and drive results is through engaging blog posts. Whether you are a seasoned blogger or just starting out, this subchapter will provide you with valuable tips and strategies to create captivating blog posts that will captivate your audience.

The key to writing engaging blog posts is to understand your audience. Take the time to research and identify the interests, needs, and pain points of your target audience. This will enable you to create content that resonates with them and addresses their specific concerns. Remember, the more relevant your content is to your audience, the more likely they are to engage with it.

Another important aspect of creating engaging blog posts is to have a compelling headline. Your headline should be attention-grabbing and pique the curiosity of your readers. Use power words, numbers, and intriguing statements to entice your audience to click and read your blog post.

Once you have captured your readers' attention with a captivating headline, it is essential to deliver high-quality content. Make sure your blog posts are well-researched, informative, and provide value to your readers. Use a conversational tone and avoid jargon to make your content more accessible and engaging.

In addition to well-written content, incorporating visual elements can significantly enhance the engagement of your blog posts. Use relevant images, infographics, and videos to break up the text and make your content more visually appealing. Visuals not only capture the attention of your readers but also help to convey your message more effectively.

Furthermore, encourage interaction with your readers by including a call to action at the end of your blog posts. This could be asking them to leave a comment, share the post on social media, or subscribe to your newsletter. By actively engaging your audience, you can build a loyal community around your blog and increase your online presence.

In conclusion, creating engaging blog posts is an essential element of a successful digital marketing strategy. By understanding your audience, crafting compelling headlines, delivering high-quality content, incorporating visual elements, and encouraging interaction, you can create blog posts that captivate your audience and drive results. So, get started today and take your digital business to new heights with engaging blog posts!

Video Marketing Strategies

In today's digital business landscape, video marketing has emerged as a powerful tool for boosting online presence and driving results. It has become an essential component of any comprehensive digital marketing strategy. Videos have the ability to capture attention, engage viewers, and effectively communicate your brand message. Whether you are a small business owner, a digital marketer, or an entrepreneur looking to make an impact, understanding and implementing effective video marketing strategies is crucial.

One of the key advantages of video marketing is its ability to convey complex information in a visually appealing and easily digestible format. With the increasing consumption of video content across various platforms, it is important to create videos that are not only entertaining but also informative and relevant to your target audience. This subchapter explores the various strategies and techniques that can help you leverage the power of video marketing to achieve your business goals.

Firstly, we delve into the importance of defining your target audience and understanding their preferences and needs. By conducting thorough market research, you can identify the type of videos that will resonate with your audience and create content that is tailored to their interests. This will ensure that your videos are more likely to be shared and generate engagement.

Next, we discuss the importance of storytelling in video marketing. Storytelling is a powerful technique that allows you to connect with your audience on an emotional level. By crafting compelling narratives and using visual elements effectively, you can create videos that leave a lasting impression and drive action.

Additionally, this subchapter explores the various platforms and channels available for video distribution, such as YouTube, social media, and email marketing. Each platform has its own unique features and audience, and understanding how to optimize your videos for each channel is crucial for maximizing their reach and impact.

Furthermore, we discuss the importance of video SEO and how to optimize your videos for search engines. By implementing relevant keywords, creating catchy titles, and optimizing video descriptions, you can increase the visibility of your videos and drive organic traffic to your website.

Finally, we delve into the analytics and metrics that can help you measure the success of your video marketing campaigns. By tracking key performance indicators such as views, engagement, and conversion rates, you can gain valuable insights into the effectiveness of your videos and make data-driven decisions to improve future campaigns.

In conclusion, video marketing is an essential component of any digital business strategy. By understanding and implementing effective video marketing strategies, you can boost your online presence, engage your audience, and drive tangible results. This subchapter provides valuable insights and practical tips to help you leverage the power of video marketing and achieve your business goals.

Infographic and Visual Content Marketing

In today's fast-paced digital business environment, where attention spans are shrinking by the second, capturing and retaining the interest of your target audience is paramount. This is where the power of visual content marketing, particularly infographics, comes into play. Infographics are a visually appealing way to convey complex information and engage with your audience effectively.

Infographics are a dynamic tool that combines concise text, compelling visuals, and data-driven insights to tell a story or present information in a visually captivating manner. They have the ability to simplify complex concepts, making them easier to understand and digest. By incorporating infographics into your marketing strategy, you can grab the attention of your audience and communicate your message quickly and efficiently.

Why are infographics so effective in the digital business world? Well, humans are visual creatures. We process and retain visual information much faster and better than plain text. In fact, studies have shown that infographics can improve information retention by up to 65%. This makes them a powerful tool for digital marketers looking to convey their message in a memorable way.

Moreover, infographics have the potential to go viral. Due to their visually appealing nature, people are more likely to share them on social media platforms, resulting in increased brand visibility and organic reach. This viral potential can significantly boost your online presence and drive traffic to your website or social media channels.

To create an effective infographic, it's crucial to have a clear understanding of your target audience and their preferences. Consider their demographics, interests, and pain points to tailor the content and design of your infographic accordingly. Keep the text concise and visually appealing, using charts, graphs, icons, and images to convey your message effectively.

Remember, the key to successful visual content marketing lies in creating shareable, informative, and visually stunning infographics. By harnessing the power of infographics, you can boost your online presence, engage with your audience, and drive results for your digital business.

In conclusion, the world of digital marketing is evolving rapidly, and infographics are at the forefront as a powerful tool for engaging with your target audience. By incorporating visually appealing infographics into your content marketing strategy, you can effectively convey complex information, boost your online presence, and drive results for your digital business. Embrace the power of infographics, and watch your brand soar to new heights in the digital landscape.

Content Distribution and Promotion

In today's digital world, having a strong online presence is essential for any business looking to thrive and succeed. However, simply creating great content is not enough. To truly make an impact and reach your target audience, you need to master the art of content distribution and promotion. This subchapter will guide you through the various strategies and techniques you can employ to effectively distribute and promote your digital business content.

One of the most important aspects of content distribution is understanding your audience and where they spend their time online. By identifying the platforms and channels that your target audience frequents, you can tailor your distribution efforts to reach them effectively. Whether it's social media platforms like Facebook, Twitter, or Instagram, or industry-specific forums and communities, understanding where your audience is active will help you focus your efforts in the right direction.

Once you have identified the platforms, it's crucial to optimize your content for each channel. Different platforms have different formats and preferences, so customizing your content for each platform will ensure maximum engagement and reach. For example, creating visually appealing graphics for Instagram, short and concise tweets for Twitter, or longer, informative posts for LinkedIn can help you effectively distribute your content across various channels.

In addition to optimizing your content for different platforms, leveraging influencers and thought leaders in your industry can significantly boost your content distribution efforts. Collaborating with influencers who have a large and engaged following can help you reach a wider audience and increase your content's visibility. Whether it's through guest blogging, influencer partnerships, or sponsored posts, leveraging the reach and credibility of influencers can drive remarkable results for your digital business.

Furthermore, don't underestimate the power of paid advertising. Platforms like Google Ads, Facebook Ads, and LinkedIn Ads offer highly targeted advertising options that can help you reach your specific audience with precision. Investing in paid advertising can provide an immediate boost to your content distribution efforts and ensure that your content reaches the right people at the right time.

Lastly, don't forget the importance of measuring and analyzing your content distribution efforts. By tracking metrics such as reach, engagement, and conversion rates, you can gain valuable insights into what strategies are working and what needs improvement. This data-driven approach will enable you to refine your content distribution and promotion strategies over time, ensuring continuous growth and success for your digital business.

In conclusion, mastering the art of content distribution and promotion is crucial for any digital business looking to boost its online presence and drive results. By understanding your audience, optimizing your content for different platforms, leveraging influencers, investing in paid advertising, and analyzing your efforts, you can effectively distribute and promote your content to reach and engage your target audience. By implementing these strategies, you will be well on your way to achieving digital marketing success.

Chapter 6: Conversion Rate Optimization

Introduction to Conversion Rate Optimization (CRO)

In today's digital business landscape, it is not enough to have a strong online presence; you need to drive tangible results. One key factor that can make or break your digital marketing efforts is your website's conversion rate. This is where Conversion Rate Optimization (CRO) comes into play.

Conversion Rate Optimization is the systematic process of increasing the percentage of website visitors who take the desired action, such as making a purchase, filling out a form, or subscribing to a newsletter. It is a fundamental component of any successful digital marketing strategy, as it directly impacts your bottom line.

This subchapter of "The Ultimate Guide to Digital Marketing: Boost Your Online Presence and Drive Results" aims to provide a comprehensive introduction to Conversion Rate Optimization for everyone in the digital business niche.

We will begin by explaining the importance of CRO and how it can impact your online business. By optimizing your conversion rate, you can maximize the return on investment (ROI) from your marketing efforts and increase your revenue without necessarily increasing your traffic.

Next, we will delve into the key components of a successful CRO strategy. This includes understanding your target audience, conducting thorough research and analysis, and implementing data-driven experiments to identify the most effective changes to your website.

We will also explore the various tools and techniques available for CRO, including A/B testing, heat mapping, and user feedback. These tools can provide valuable insights into user behavior and help you optimize your website's design, layout, content, and call-to-action (CTA) elements.

Furthermore, we will discuss the common pitfalls and challenges in CRO and provide tips on how to overcome them. It is crucial to avoid common mistakes and adopt a continuous improvement mindset to achieve long-term success in optimizing your conversion rate.

By the end of this subchapter, you will have a solid understanding of Conversion Rate Optimization and its importance in driving results for your digital business. You will be equipped with the knowledge and tools necessary to start optimizing your website for higher conversions and ultimately boost your online presence.

Whether you are a seasoned digital marketer or just starting out in the world of online business, this subchapter will serve as a valuable resource to help you achieve your conversion goals and drive success in the ever-evolving digital landscape.

Understanding User Experience (UX) Design

In today's digital business landscape, user experience (UX) design has become a critical component for success. As businesses strive to boost their online presence and drive results, understanding and implementing effective UX design principles can make all the difference.

So, what exactly is UX design? Simply put, it is the process of enhancing user satisfaction by improving the usability, accessibility, and enjoyment of a digital product or service. UX design focuses on creating meaningful and relevant experiences for users, ensuring that their interactions with a website, app, or any other digital platform are seamless and intuitive.

For every digital business, UX design is crucial for several reasons. First and foremost, it helps in building trust and credibility. When users have a positive experience while interacting with a website or app, they are more likely to trust the brand and its offerings. On the other hand, a poor UX can lead to frustration, negative reviews, and ultimately, loss of customers.

Moreover, UX design plays a significant role in customer retention and loyalty. By understanding user needs, preferences, and behaviors, businesses can tailor their digital platforms to provide a personalized and delightful experience. This not only encourages users to stay longer but also increases the chances of repeat visits and conversions.

To create an exceptional user experience, businesses need to consider various aspects of UX design. This includes conducting thorough user research to gain insights into their target audience, defining user personas and user journeys, and designing intuitive interfaces that are easy to navigate. Furthermore, usability testing and continuous improvement are essential to ensure that the digital product or service meets the evolving needs and expectations of users.

In the ever-evolving digital landscape, businesses cannot afford to ignore the importance of UX design. It is not only about aesthetics but also about creating a seamless and enjoyable experience for users. By understanding and implementing effective UX design principles, businesses can enhance their online presence, drive results, and ultimately, succeed in the digital marketplace.

Whether you are a seasoned digital marketer, an entrepreneur starting your own business, or simply someone interested in the world of digital business, understanding UX design is crucial. This subchapter aims to provide you with the fundamental knowledge and insights into UX design principles, allowing you to create exceptional digital experiences that resonate with your target audience. So, let's dive in and explore the fascinating world of user experience design!

A/B Testing and Multivariate Testing

In the ever-evolving world of digital business, it is crucial to stay ahead of the competition by constantly improving your online presence and driving results. One powerful tool that can help you achieve this is A/B testing and multivariate testing. These techniques allow you to experiment with different variations of your website or digital marketing campaigns to identify the most effective strategies for attracting and engaging your target audience.

A/B testing involves creating two or more versions of a webpage, email, or advertisement and randomly showing them to different segments of your audience. By tracking user behavior and analyzing the data, you can determine which version performs better in terms of conversion rates, click-through rates, or any other key performance indicators (KPIs) that align with your business goals. This iterative process of testing and refining allows you to make data-driven decisions and optimize your digital marketing efforts for maximum impact.

Multivariate testing takes A/B testing to the next level by simultaneously testing multiple variations of different elements on a webpage or within a campaign. For example, you can test different headlines, images, call-to-action buttons, and layouts to identify the winning combination that resonates most with your audience. By testing multiple variables at once, you can uncover valuable insights about the interactions between different elements and fine-tune your digital strategies accordingly.

The benefits of A/B testing and multivariate testing are numerous. Firstly, these techniques provide concrete evidence and eliminate guesswork, enabling you to make informed decisions based on real user data rather than subjective opinions. Secondly, they save you time and money by preventing you from investing resources into ineffective strategies. Instead, you can focus your efforts on the variations that have proven to be successful. Lastly, A/B testing and multivariate testing foster a culture of continuous improvement, encouraging you to regularly experiment and optimize your digital marketing efforts for better results.

To effectively implement A/B testing and multivariate testing, it is important to have a clear understanding of your business goals and target audience. Define the specific KPIs you want to improve and develop hypotheses about the variations that may lead to better outcomes. Use reliable testing tools and platforms to set up experiments, collect data, and analyze results. Remember to test one variable at a time to accurately attribute any changes in performance. Lastly, be patient and give your tests enough time to reach statistically significant results.

In conclusion, A/B testing and multivariate testing are essential tools for digital business success. By experimenting with different variations and analyzing user data, you can optimize your online presence, drive results, and stay ahead of the competition. Embrace the power of data-driven decision-making and continuously test, refine, and improve your digital marketing strategies for maximum impact.

Landing Page Optimization

In the fast-paced world of digital business, one thing is abundantly clear - your online presence can make or break your success. With countless websites vying for attention, it is crucial to optimize every aspect of your digital marketing strategy, starting with your landing pages.

A landing page serves as the gateway to your website or online business. It is the first impression you make on potential customers, and it can significantly impact your conversion rates. To ensure you are making the most of this crucial opportunity, landing page optimization is essential.

Landing page optimization involves fine-tuning various elements to create a seamless user experience that drives results. By focusing on key aspects such as design, messaging, and usability, you can increase the chances of capturing visitors' attention and converting them into loyal customers.

One of the primary objectives of landing page optimization is to enhance the overall design. A visually appealing and user-friendly layout can significantly impact visitors' impression of your brand. A cluttered or confusing design can quickly turn potential customers away. By employing a clean and intuitive design, you can guide visitors through your page, making it easier for them to find the information they are looking for.

Another crucial aspect of landing page optimization is crafting compelling messaging. Your landing page should clearly communicate your unique value proposition and highlight the benefits visitors can expect from engaging with your business. Powerful headlines, persuasive copy, and captivating visuals can all work together to create a convincing argument for visitors to take the desired action.

Usability is another critical factor to consider when optimizing landing pages. A seamless user experience ensures that visitors can easily navigate your page, find relevant information, and complete desired actions, such as signing up for a newsletter or making a purchase. By removing any unnecessary steps or barriers, you can streamline the user journey, increasing the likelihood of conversions.

In conclusion, landing page optimization is a vital component of any successful digital business. By focusing on design, messaging, and usability, you can create a compelling and seamless user experience that drives results. Remember, your landing page is often the first impression potential customers have of your brand, so make it count. By investing time and effort into optimizing this crucial aspect of your online presence, you can boost your conversion rates, increase customer engagement, and ultimately drive the success of your digital business.

Call-to-Action (CTA) Optimization

In the fast-paced world of digital business, it's not enough to have a stunning website or a strong online presence. You need to actively drive results and convert your website visitors into customers. This is where Call-to-Action (CTA) optimization comes into play.

A Call-to-Action is a powerful tool that prompts your audience to take a specific action. It could be anything from signing up for a newsletter, making a purchase, or downloading a free ebook. By optimizing your CTAs, you can significantly increase your conversion rates and drive more revenue for your digital business.

So, how can you optimize your CTAs to achieve maximum results?

First and foremost, your CTA should be clear and compelling. Use action-oriented language that creates a sense of urgency and motivates your audience to take action. Words like "buy now," "sign up today," or "get started" can make a significant impact on your conversion rates.

Next, make sure your CTA stands out visually. Use contrasting colors and bold fonts to draw attention to your CTA button. It should be easily noticeable and stand out from the rest of your website's design. Additionally, consider the placement of your CTA. It should be strategically positioned above the fold, where it's visible without requiring scrolling.

Another essential aspect of CTA optimization is personalization. Tailor your CTAs to specific audience segments based on their interests, demographics, or browsing behavior. By showing relevant

CTAs to different groups of people, you can enhance their user experience and increase the chances of conversion.

Furthermore, it's crucial to test and analyze the performance of your CTAs regularly. A/B testing can help you determine which CTAs are driving the most conversions. Experiment with different designs, colors, copy, and placements to find the most effective combination for your audience.

Finally, don't forget to optimize your CTAs for mobile users. With the increasing use of smartphones and tablets, a significant portion of your audience accesses your website through mobile devices. Ensure that your CTAs are mobile-friendly, easily clickable, and properly displayed on smaller screens.

By implementing these CTA optimization strategies, you can boost your online presence and drive tangible results for your digital business. Remember, the key is to continuously test, analyze, and refine your CTAs to ensure maximum effectiveness. So, go ahead, optimize your CTAs, and watch your conversion rates soar!

Chapter 7: Analytics and Reporting

Introduction to Analytics and Reporting

In today's digital business landscape, understanding analytics and reporting is crucial to effectively boost your online presence and drive results. Whether you are a small business owner, a marketer, or simply someone interested in the world of digital marketing, this subchapter will provide you with a comprehensive introduction to analytics and reporting.

Analytics refers to the process of collecting and analyzing data to gain insights into various aspects of your online presence. It allows you to measure the performance of your digital marketing efforts, understand your target audience, and make informed decisions to optimize your strategies.

The first step in leveraging analytics is to determine which metrics are relevant to your digital business. Depending on your specific goals and objectives, you may focus on metrics such as website traffic, conversion rates, social media engagement, or email open rates. By tracking these metrics over time, you will gain valuable insights into the effectiveness of your digital marketing campaigns and identify areas for improvement.

Reporting, on the other hand, involves presenting the analyzed data in a clear and concise manner. It enables you to communicate the performance of your digital marketing efforts to stakeholders, including clients, managers, or team members. Effective reporting should be visually appealing, contain relevant data, and provide actionable recommendations.

To make the most of analytics and reporting, it is crucial to use the right tools. There are numerous analytics platforms available that can help you collect and analyze data, such as Google Analytics, Adobe Analytics, or HubSpot. These tools provide a wealth of information about your website visitors, their behavior, and the effectiveness of your marketing campaigns.

Moreover, it is essential to regularly monitor and review your analytics data. By doing so, you can identify trends, spot anomalies, and make data-driven decisions to improve your digital marketing strategies. It is recommended to set up regular reporting intervals, such as weekly or monthly, to keep track of your progress and make necessary adjustments.

In conclusion, analytics and reporting play a vital role in the success of any digital business. By understanding and utilizing these tools effectively, you can gain valuable insights, optimize your online presence, and drive tangible results. Stay tuned as we dive deeper into specific analytics metrics and reporting techniques in the following chapters of this book.

Key Metrics in Digital Marketing

In today's digital age, it is essential for businesses to have a strong online presence in order to stay competitive. Digital marketing has become a powerful tool that can help businesses reach a wider audience and drive tangible results. However, in order to make the most of digital marketing strategies, it is important to understand and track key metrics that can provide valuable insights into the effectiveness of your campaigns. In this subchapter, we will explore some of the key metrics in digital marketing that every business should be aware of.

1. Website Traffic: This metric measures the number of visitors to your website. It is crucial to monitor your website traffic as it gives you an idea of how many people are interested in your products or services. By analyzing website traffic, you can identify which marketing channels are driving the most visitors to your site and make informed decisions on where to allocate your marketing budget.

2. Conversion Rate: Conversion rate measures the percentage of website visitors who take a desired action, such as making a purchase or filling out a form. This metric helps you evaluate the effectiveness of your landing pages and marketing campaigns. A high conversion rate indicates that your website and marketing efforts are resonating with your target audience.

3. Cost per Acquisition (CPA): CPA measures the cost required to acquire a new customer. It is calculated by dividing the total cost of your marketing campaigns by the number of new customers acquired.

By tracking CPA, you can determine if your marketing campaigns are cost-effective and adjust your strategies accordingly.

4. Return on Investment (ROI): ROI measures the profitability of your marketing campaigns. It compares the revenue generated from your marketing efforts to the cost of those efforts. ROI enables you to evaluate the effectiveness of your marketing campaigns and allocate your resources wisely.

5. Customer Lifetime Value (CLV): CLV measures the total revenue a customer is expected to generate over the course of their relationship with your business. By calculating CLV, you can identify your most valuable customers and tailor your marketing strategies to retain and attract similar customers.

Tracking these key metrics is crucial for any digital business. They provide valuable insights into the effectiveness of your marketing efforts and enable you to make data-driven decisions. By understanding and optimizing these metrics, you can boost your online presence and drive tangible results in the digital marketplace.

In conclusion, digital marketing is a powerful tool for businesses to reach a wider audience and drive results. By tracking key metrics such as website traffic, conversion rate, CPA, ROI, and CLV, businesses can gain valuable insights into the effectiveness of their marketing campaigns. These metrics allow businesses to make data-driven decisions and optimize their strategies to boost their online presence and drive tangible results in the digital marketplace.

Using Google Analytics for Tracking and Analysis

In today's digital business landscape, it is crucial to have a strong online presence in order to drive results and stay ahead of the competition. One of the most powerful tools available to digital businesses is Google Analytics, a comprehensive platform that provides invaluable insights into website performance and user behavior. Whether you are a small startup or an established enterprise, harnessing the power of Google Analytics can greatly enhance your online marketing efforts and help you make data-driven decisions.

Google Analytics offers a wide range of features that allow you to track and analyze various aspects of your website and marketing campaigns. From monitoring website traffic and user engagement to measuring conversion rates and identifying the most effective channels for driving traffic, Google Analytics provides a wealth of information that can drive your digital business forward.

One of the key benefits of using Google Analytics is the ability to track website traffic and gain a deeper understanding of your audience. The platform allows you to monitor the number of visitors to your site, their geographic location, the devices they are using, and even their browsing behavior. Armed with this information, you can tailor your marketing strategies to target specific demographics and optimize your website for better user experience.

Furthermore, Google Analytics enables you to track the performance of your marketing campaigns. Whether you are running paid advertising campaigns or implementing search engine optimization techniques, Google Analytics provides detailed reports on the effectiveness of your efforts. You can track key metrics such as click-through rates, conversion rates, and return on investment to identify which strategies are delivering the best results and make adjustments accordingly.

Another valuable feature of Google Analytics is the ability to set up goals and track conversions. By defining specific actions that you want users to take on your website, such as making a purchase or subscribing to a newsletter, you can easily measure how well your website is converting visitors into customers. This data can help you identify areas for improvement and optimize your website to increase conversions.

In conclusion, Google Analytics is an essential tool for digital businesses looking to boost their online presence and drive results. By utilizing its powerful tracking and analysis capabilities, you can gain valuable insights into your website performance, user behavior, and marketing campaigns. Armed with this knowledge, you can make informed decisions to optimize your digital marketing efforts and ultimately achieve your business goals.

Social Media Analytics and Insights

In today's digital business landscape, social media has become an integral part of every organization's marketing strategy. It has transformed the way businesses connect with their customers, build brand awareness, and drive sales. However, simply having a presence on social media platforms is not enough. To truly harness the power of social media, it is essential to understand the analytics and insights that can be derived from these platforms.

Social media analytics refers to the process of collecting and analyzing data from various social media channels to gain valuable insights about audience behavior, content performance, and overall campaign effectiveness. By leveraging this data, businesses can make informed decisions, optimize their marketing efforts, and achieve better results.

One of the key benefits of social media analytics is the ability to track and measure the impact of your social media activities. With the right tools and techniques, you can monitor the reach and engagement of your posts, identify trends, and understand which content resonates most with your target audience. This valuable information can help you tailor your content strategy and deliver more relevant and impactful messages to your followers.

Moreover, social media analytics allows you to gain a deeper understanding of your audience demographics, interests, and preferences. By analyzing this data, you can create buyer personas and develop targeted marketing campaigns that are more likely to resonate with your ideal customers. This level of personalization can significantly improve the effectiveness of your marketing efforts and drive higher conversion rates.

Another crucial aspect of social media analytics is sentiment analysis. By monitoring the sentiment surrounding your brand or industry on social media, you can gauge public opinion, identify potential issues, and respond proactively to any negative feedback or customer concerns. This real-time feedback loop enables you to maintain a positive brand image and build stronger customer relationships.

In conclusion, social media analytics and insights are indispensable tools for any digital business looking to boost their online presence and drive results. By harnessing the power of data, businesses can optimize their social media strategies, deliver more personalized experiences, and make informed decisions that positively impact their bottom line. Whether you are a small startup or a multinational corporation, understanding social media analytics is essential for staying competitive in today's digital landscape.

Reporting on ROI and Campaign Performance

Title: Reporting on ROI and Campaign Performance

Introduction:
In today's digital business landscape, measuring the return on investment (ROI) and campaign performance is crucial for driving results and boosting your online presence. This subchapter aims to equip every digital business professional with the knowledge and tools necessary to effectively report on ROI and campaign performance. By understanding these metrics, you will be able to make data-driven decisions, optimize your marketing strategies, and achieve greater success in the online world.

Understanding ROI:
Return on Investment (ROI) is a fundamental metric that quantifies the profitability of your marketing efforts. It determines the success of your campaigns by comparing the revenue generated against the costs incurred. Digital businesses must accurately calculate ROI to justify their marketing spend and identify areas for improvement. This section will explain the formula for calculating ROI and delve into different attribution models, such as first click, last click, and multi-touch attribution.

Key Performance Indicators (KPIs):
To assess campaign performance, it is vital to track and analyze various Key Performance Indicators (KPIs). KPIs provide valuable insights into the effectiveness of your marketing campaigns and allow you to benchmark your performance against set goals. This subchapter will cover essential KPIs specific to digital business, including click-

through rates (CTR), conversion rates, customer acquisition costs (CAC), and customer lifetime value (CLV). By monitoring these metrics, you can optimize your campaigns and drive better results.

Data Visualization and Reporting Tools: Effectively reporting on ROI and campaign performance requires powerful data visualization and reporting tools. This section will introduce you to a variety of tools that simplify the process of collecting, analyzing, and presenting data. From Google Analytics to advanced marketing automation platforms, you will learn how to leverage these tools to create comprehensive reports that provide actionable insights. We will also discuss the importance of data visualization techniques to communicate complex information in a clear and visually appealing manner.

Optimizing Campaigns Based on Reports: Once you have collected and analyzed the data, it's time to optimize your campaigns based on the insights gained. This subchapter will guide you through the process of leveraging your reports to identify trends, uncover opportunities, and make data-driven adjustments. Whether it's refining your target audience, adjusting ad copy, or reallocating your budget, you will learn how to make informed decisions that maximize your ROI and campaign performance.

Conclusion:

Reporting on ROI and campaign performance is the cornerstone of digital marketing success. By understanding and effectively utilizing these metrics, digital business professionals can optimize their strategies, drive results, and boost their online presence. This subchapter has provided the necessary knowledge and tools to measure ROI, track KPIs, leverage data visualization and reporting tools, and optimize campaigns based on the insights gained. Armed with these skills, you are well-equipped to navigate the digital landscape and achieve your business objectives.

Chapter 8: Mobile Marketing

Introduction to Mobile Marketing

In today's digital age, mobile devices have become an integral part of our daily lives. As smartphones and tablets continue to dominate the market, businesses have recognized the immense potential of reaching out to their target audience through mobile marketing. Mobile marketing refers to the practice of promoting products and services to users on their mobile devices such as smartphones and tablets. This subchapter aims to provide an introduction to mobile marketing and its significance in the world of digital business.

Mobile marketing offers a unique opportunity for businesses to connect with their customers on a more personal and immediate level. With the majority of people now using their smartphones for browsing the internet, shopping, and even making payments, it is crucial for businesses to optimize their marketing strategies to cater to this growing trend.

One of the key advantages of mobile marketing is its ability to reach a wider audience. Unlike traditional marketing methods, mobile marketing allows businesses to target specific demographics, locations, and interests, allowing for more precise and effective campaigns. By leveraging mobile apps, SMS marketing, mobile-friendly websites, and social media platforms, businesses can engage with their customers in real-time, providing personalized offers, discounts, and updates.

Furthermore, mobile marketing enables businesses to create a seamless and integrated customer experience. By utilizing location-based services, businesses can deliver hyper-localized advertisements and promotions, increasing the chances of conversion. Additionally, mobile marketing can be seamlessly integrated with other digital marketing channels such as email marketing and social media, ensuring a cohesive and consistent brand presence across all platforms.

However, to succeed in mobile marketing, businesses need to be aware of the evolving trends and technologies in this rapidly changing landscape. From responsive web design to mobile apps and augmented reality, staying updated with the latest advancements is paramount. Moreover, businesses need to prioritize user experience by ensuring their websites and apps are mobile-friendly, easy to navigate, and load quickly.

In conclusion, mobile marketing is a crucial aspect of digital business in today's fast-paced world. By embracing mobile marketing strategies, businesses can effectively reach their target audience, provide personalized experiences, and drive meaningful results. This subchapter will delve deeper into various mobile marketing tactics, best practices, and case studies to equip readers with the knowledge and tools to enhance their online presence and drive success in the digital realm.

Mobile Advertising Strategies

In today's digital age, mobile advertising has become an essential component of any successful marketing strategy. With smartphones becoming an integral part of our daily lives, businesses must adapt and optimize their advertising efforts to reach their target audience effectively. This subchapter aims to provide a comprehensive understanding of mobile advertising strategies and how they can help boost your online presence and drive results for your digital business.

1. Understanding Mobile Advertising: To start, it is crucial to grasp the fundamentals of mobile advertising. This section will introduce the concept of mobile advertising, its benefits, and the various types of mobile ads available, such as banner ads, interstitial ads, native ads, and video ads. By understanding these different formats, you can choose the most suitable ones for your digital business.

2. Targeting the Right Audience: One of the significant advantages of mobile advertising is the ability to target specific demographics and interests. This section will delve into the importance of audience segmentation and how to identify your target audience. By effectively targeting the right audience, you can maximize your ad's impact and return on investment.

3. Optimizing for Mobile Devices: Mobile advertising requires a unique approach compared to traditional desktop advertising. This section will explore the importance of optimizing your ads for mobile devices, including considerations such as responsive design, load times, and user experience. By ensuring your ads are mobile-friendly, you can enhance engagement and conversion rates.

4. Leveraging Mobile Apps: With the proliferation of mobile apps, this section will discuss the opportunities and strategies to advertise within popular mobile applications. From in-app ads to sponsored content, you will learn how to leverage mobile apps to reach your target audience effectively and drive results for your digital business.

5. Utilizing Location-Based Advertising: Mobile devices provide valuable location data that can be utilized for targeted advertising. This section will explore location-based advertising strategies, including geofencing, beacon technology, and hyper-local targeting. By incorporating location-based ads, you can deliver relevant content to users in specific geographic areas, driving foot traffic and boosting online sales.

6. Measuring and Analyzing Results: No advertising strategy is complete without proper measurement and analysis. This section will guide you on how to track and measure the success of your mobile advertising campaigns. From click-through rates to conversion tracking, you will learn how to optimize your campaigns based on real-time data and drive better results.

In conclusion, mobile advertising is a critical component of any digital business's marketing strategy. By understanding the various mobile advertising strategies and implementing them effectively, you can boost your online presence, reach your target audience, and drive significant results for your digital business.

App Store Optimization (ASO)

In today's digital world, where mobile apps have become an integral part of our lives, app store optimization (ASO) has emerged as a crucial strategy for businesses looking to boost their online presence and drive results. Whether you are a seasoned digital marketer or a digital business owner, understanding the concepts and techniques of ASO is essential to maximize the visibility and success of your mobile app.

ASO refers to the process of optimizing an app's visibility and ranking in the various app stores, such as Google Play Store and Apple App Store. Just like search engine optimization (SEO) for websites, ASO aims to improve the app's organic search rankings, increase downloads, and ultimately enhance user engagement and retention.

One of the primary goals of ASO is to increase the visibility of your app in app store search results. To achieve this, it is crucial to conduct thorough keyword research and strategically incorporate relevant keywords in your app's title, description, and other metadata. By using the right keywords, you can ensure that your app appears in relevant search queries, driving more organic traffic and potential users.

Another significant aspect of ASO is optimizing your app's visual elements. The app icon, screenshots, and preview videos play a critical role in attracting users' attention and convincing them to download your app. A visually appealing and informative app page can significantly impact the conversion rate and increase downloads.

Furthermore, user reviews and ratings have a profound influence on app store rankings. Encouraging satisfied users to leave positive reviews and addressing any negative feedback promptly can help improve your app's reputation and credibility. It is essential to actively engage with your users and provide regular updates to keep them satisfied and loyal.

ASO is an ongoing process that requires constant monitoring and optimization. Regularly analyzing app store metrics, such as download rates, conversion rates, and user behavior, can provide valuable insights into the effectiveness of your ASO strategies. By continuously tweaking and improving your app's optimization, you can stay ahead of the competition and drive long-term success.

In conclusion, ASO is a vital component of any digital business's marketing strategy. By implementing effective ASO techniques, you can enhance your app's visibility, increase organic downloads, and ultimately drive better results. Whether you are a digital marketer or a business owner, understanding and implementing ASO is crucial to staying competitive in the ever-evolving world of mobile apps.

Mobile-Friendly Website Design

In today's digital age, having a mobile-friendly website is no longer a luxury, but a necessity for any business aiming to thrive in the online world. With the increasing use of smartphones and tablets, more and more people are accessing the internet on their mobile devices. As a result, businesses must adapt their website design to cater to this growing trend if they want to remain relevant and competitive.

A mobile-friendly website refers to a website that is specifically designed and optimized for seamless viewing and navigation on mobile devices. It ensures that users have a positive experience when accessing the website on their smartphones or tablets, with easy-to-read text, properly sized images, and user-friendly navigation.

One of the primary benefits of having a mobile-friendly website is improved user experience. Mobile users typically have different needs and behaviors compared to desktop users. They are often on the go, seeking quick information or completing tasks in a shorter timeframe. A mobile-friendly website caters to these preferences by providing a streamlined and efficient user experience, allowing visitors to find what they need effortlessly.

Moreover, mobile-friendly website design positively impacts search engine optimization (SEO). Search engines like Google prioritize mobile-friendly websites in their search results, as they recognize the importance of delivering a positive user experience. By having a mobile-friendly website, businesses increase their chances of ranking higher in search engine results pages, driving more organic traffic to their site.

Furthermore, a mobile-friendly website design is crucial for digital businesses. Online shopping and e-commerce have skyrocketed in recent years, with a significant portion of purchases being made through mobile devices. To capture this growing market, digital businesses must ensure their websites are optimized for mobile commerce, providing a seamless shopping experience that encourages conversions and sales.

In conclusion, a mobile-friendly website design is essential for any business operating in the digital sphere. It improves user experience, enhances search engine visibility, and is crucial for digital businesses aiming to capture the mobile commerce market. By investing in mobile-friendly website design, businesses can boost their online presence, drive results, and stay ahead in the ever-evolving world of digital marketing.

SMS Marketing

In today's fast-paced digital world, staying connected with your audience is paramount for any digital business. With the rise of smartphones and the constant use of text messaging, SMS marketing has become a powerful tool to boost your online presence and drive results. This subchapter will provide you with a comprehensive understanding of SMS marketing and how you can leverage its potential to reach a wider audience.

SMS marketing, also known as text message marketing, involves sending promotional messages or alerts to your customers via SMS. It is an effective and cost-efficient way to engage with your audience, as nearly everyone owns a mobile phone. Unlike emails or social media posts, SMS marketing offers a direct and immediate connection with your customers.

One of the key advantages of SMS marketing is its high open and response rates. Studies have shown that SMS messages have a staggering 98% open rate within the first three minutes of delivery. This means that your message will likely be seen by your audience, ensuring higher engagement and conversions.

To make the most of SMS marketing, it is crucial to build a permission-based subscriber list. This means obtaining explicit consent from your customers to receive SMS messages from your business. You can encourage sign-ups by offering exclusive discounts, updates, or valuable content that your audience cannot resist.

Once you have a subscriber list, it's essential to craft compelling and concise messages that resonate with your audience. SMS messages have a character limit, usually around 160 characters, so make every word count. Focus on offering value, whether it's announcing limited-time offers, promoting new products, or sharing exclusive content.

Personalization is another crucial aspect of SMS marketing. Address your customers by their names and tailor the content to their preferences and past interactions. This level of personalization will make your audience feel valued and increase the likelihood of conversion.

Furthermore, timing plays a vital role in SMS marketing. Avoid sending messages during late hours or busy times when your audience might be less receptive. Experiment with different timings and track the response rates to determine the optimal time to send your messages.

Lastly, don't forget to track and analyze your SMS marketing campaigns. Use analytics tools to measure the effectiveness of your messages, click-through rates, and conversion rates. This data will provide valuable insights into your audience's behavior and help you refine your future SMS marketing strategies.

In conclusion, SMS marketing is a powerful tool for any digital business to boost their online presence and drive results. By building a permission-based subscriber list, crafting compelling messages, personalizing content, optimizing timing, and tracking campaign performance, you can effectively engage with your audience and achieve your marketing goals. Stay connected with your customers through SMS marketing, and watch your online presence soar.

Chapter 9: Influencer Marketing

Introduction to Influencer Marketing

In today's digital business landscape, where competition is fierce and attention spans are short, traditional marketing strategies alone are no longer sufficient to boost your online presence and drive results. Enter influencer marketing – a powerful and effective tactic that has taken the digital world by storm.

In this subchapter, we will dive into the exciting world of influencer marketing and explore how it can revolutionize your digital business. Whether you're a seasoned marketer or just starting out, understanding influencer marketing is crucial to stay ahead of the curve and connect with your target audience in a meaningful way.

So, what exactly is influencer marketing? At its core, it involves leveraging the influence and reach of popular individuals, known as influencers, to promote your brand, products, or services. These influencers have built a loyal following on various social media platforms, such as Instagram, YouTube, or TikTok, and possess the ability to affect the purchasing decisions of their audience. By collaborating with influencers who align with your brand values and target audience, you can tap into their credibility and authority to drive awareness, engagement, and ultimately, conversions.

One of the key advantages of influencer marketing is its ability to create authentic and relatable content. Unlike traditional advertising, which can feel forced or intrusive, influencer-generated content is seamlessly integrated into the influencer's own content style, making it more genuine and trustworthy. This authenticity resonates with consumers, leading to higher engagement rates and increased brand loyalty.

In this subchapter, we will explore various aspects of influencer marketing, including finding the right influencers for your brand, establishing successful partnerships, and measuring the effectiveness of your campaigns. We will also delve into the different types of influencer marketing, such as sponsored posts, product reviews, and influencer takeovers, and provide insights on how to create compelling content that aligns with your brand message.

Additionally, we will discuss the potential challenges and pitfalls of influencer marketing, such as fake influencers or controversies, and provide strategies to mitigate these risks. It's crucial to approach influencer marketing with a well-thought-out strategy, clear objectives, and a thorough understanding of the legal and ethical considerations involved.

Whether you're looking to promote your digital business, increase brand awareness, or drive sales, influencer marketing can be a game-changer. By harnessing the power of influential individuals, you can amplify your online presence, connect with your target audience on a deeper level, and ultimately achieve remarkable results.

So, fasten your seatbelts as we embark on this journey into the world of influencer marketing. Get ready to learn, explore, and discover the endless possibilities that await you in this exciting realm of digital marketing.

Identifying and Collaborating with Influencers

In today's digital business landscape, influencers have become a powerful force in driving brand awareness and consumer engagement. Collaborating with influencers can significantly boost your online presence and drive results like never before. Whether you are a small start-up or an established company, understanding how to identify and collaborate with influencers is crucial for your success.

But first, what exactly is an influencer? An influencer is an individual or organization with a large and engaged following on social media platforms. They have established credibility, expertise, and trust within a specific niche, making them influential in shaping consumer opinions and behaviors.

To begin the process of identifying influencers, start by defining your target audience and understanding their interests. Research different social media platforms and identify influencers who align with your niche and have a substantial following. Tools like BuzzSumo and Hootsuite can help you find influencers based on keywords and specific industry categories.

Once you have identified potential influencers, it's essential to evaluate their credibility and authenticity. Look for influencers who have a genuine connection with their audience and consistently produce high-quality content. Consider factors such as engagement rates, audience demographics, and the influencer's overall reputation.

When it comes to collaborating with influencers, it's crucial to approach them with a well-thought-out strategy. Begin by building a relationship with them – engage with their content, share their posts, and genuinely show interest in their work. Once you have established a connection, reach out to them with a personalized pitch, highlighting how your brand aligns with their values and offering a mutually beneficial partnership.

Collaboration opportunities with influencers can vary. It could be a sponsored post, a product review, a giveaway, or even a guest blog post. Ensure that the collaboration is authentic and adds value to both the influencer's audience and your brand. Remember, the goal is to create content that resonates with the influencer's followers and drives meaningful engagement.

Furthermore, it's essential to set clear expectations and guidelines for the collaboration. Be transparent about your goals, budget, and desired outcomes. Establish a timeline and ensure that both parties are on the same page regarding deliverables, content approvals, and performance metrics.

In conclusion, identifying and collaborating with influencers is a powerful strategy for boosting your online presence and driving results in the digital business world. By understanding your target audience, researching potential influencers, and building authentic relationships, you can create impactful collaborations that amplify your brand's visibility and credibility. Embrace the influence of influencers and unlock new opportunities for growth in the digital marketing realm.

Creating Effective Influencer Marketing Campaigns

In today's digital business landscape, influencer marketing has emerged as a powerful tool to boost your online presence and drive results. Collaborating with influential individuals who have a substantial following can help you connect with your target audience in an authentic and engaging way. However, to ensure the success of your influencer marketing campaigns, it is crucial to follow a systematic approach that aligns with your goals and values.

1. Define Your Objectives: Before diving into influencer marketing, clearly define your objectives. Are you aiming to increase brand awareness, drive traffic to your website, or boost sales? Understanding your goals will help you identify the right influencers and design campaigns that resonate with your target audience.

2. Identify Your Target Audience: To create effective influencer marketing campaigns, you need to know who your target audience is. Research and analyze their demographics, interests, and preferences. By understanding their needs, you can find influencers whose content aligns with your brand and appeals to your audience.

3. Find the Right Influencers: Finding the right influencers is crucial for the success of your campaigns. Look for influencers who align with your brand values, have a genuine following, and create content that resonates with your target audience. Use social media platforms, influencer marketing tools, and agencies to identify potential influencers.

4. Establish Authentic Relationships: Building authentic relationships with influencers is essential. Engage with their content, comment on their posts, and share their work to establish a genuine connection. Once you have established a relationship, communicate your brand values and campaign goals clearly, ensuring the influencer understands your expectations.

5. Collaborate on Creative Campaigns: Develop creative campaigns that allow influencers to showcase your brand in an authentic way. Encourage them to incorporate your products or services into their content creatively. Give influencers creative freedom, as their unique perspective can have a significant impact on your target audience.

6. Track and Measure Results: To gauge the success of your influencer marketing campaigns, track and measure key metrics such as engagement, reach, website traffic, and conversions. Use analytics tools and platform insights to analyze the performance of your campaigns and make data-driven decisions for future collaborations.

Influencer marketing has the power to amplify your digital business and drive tangible results. By following these steps and continually refining your approach, you can create effective influencer marketing campaigns that successfully connect with your target audience, boost your online presence, and drive meaningful results.

Measuring the Success of Influencer Marketing

In the fast-paced world of digital marketing, influencer marketing has emerged as a powerful tool for businesses to boost their online presence and drive results. With the rise of social media platforms, influencers have gained significant popularity and influence among consumers. As a result, businesses of all sizes and industries are increasingly turning to influencers to promote their products or services.

But how can you measure the success of your influencer marketing campaigns? In this subchapter, we will explore various metrics and strategies to help you gauge the effectiveness of your influencer partnerships and ensure you are getting the most out of your digital marketing efforts.

One of the most important metrics to consider is reach. Reach refers to the number of people who have been exposed to your influencer's content. Social media platforms provide valuable insights into the number of followers, likes, shares, and comments an influencer receives. By analyzing these metrics, you can assess the potential reach of your campaign and determine if it aligns with your target audience.

Engagement is another critical factor in measuring the success of influencer marketing. It goes beyond reach and focuses on how your audience interacts with the content. Are they liking, commenting, or sharing the posts? By tracking engagement metrics, such as the number of likes, comments, and shares, you can assess the level of interest and connection your influencer's content generates.

Conversion rate is a key indicator of the effectiveness of your influencer marketing campaigns. It measures the number of people who take a desired action after seeing the influencer's content, such as making a purchase, signing up for a newsletter, or downloading an e-book. By setting up trackable links or using unique promo codes, you can easily attribute conversions to your influencer's efforts.

Additionally, monitoring brand sentiment is crucial to understanding the impact of influencer marketing on your digital business. Are people talking positively or negatively about your brand after seeing the influencer's content? Analyzing sentiment through social listening tools can help you gauge the overall perception of your brand and identify areas for improvement.

In conclusion, measuring the success of influencer marketing requires a comprehensive analysis of reach, engagement, conversion rate, and brand sentiment. By effectively tracking these metrics, you can evaluate the impact of your influencer partnerships and make data-driven decisions to optimize your digital marketing strategies.

Chapter 10: E-commerce Marketing

Introduction to E-commerce Marketing

In today's digital age, where technology is rapidly advancing, businesses are constantly seeking new and innovative ways to enhance their online presence and drive results. One of the most effective strategies for achieving this is through e-commerce marketing. This subchapter serves as an introduction to e-commerce marketing, providing valuable insights and guidance for individuals, entrepreneurs, and businesses operating in the digital business niche.

E-commerce marketing refers to the strategic implementation of marketing techniques specifically tailored for online businesses. It encompasses a wide range of activities aimed at attracting, engaging, and converting potential customers into loyal buyers. By leveraging digital platforms and tools, businesses can reach a global audience, increase brand visibility, and ultimately drive sales and revenue.

In this subchapter, we will delve into the fundamental concepts of e-commerce marketing. We will explore the various components that make up a successful e-commerce marketing strategy, including search engine optimization (SEO), social media marketing, email marketing, content marketing, and paid advertising. By understanding these essential elements, individuals and businesses can develop a comprehensive marketing plan to effectively promote their products or services in the digital marketplace.

Moreover, we will discuss the importance of market research and understanding consumer behavior in e-commerce marketing. By analyzing industry trends, identifying target audiences, and crafting buyer personas, businesses can tailor their marketing messages and offerings to meet the specific needs and preferences of their customers.

Furthermore, we will explore the significance of user experience and website optimization in e-commerce marketing. A well-designed website that is easy to navigate, visually appealing, and mobile-friendly plays a crucial role in attracting and retaining customers. We will provide practical tips and strategies for optimizing websites for better conversion rates and customer satisfaction.

Additionally, this subchapter will touch on the emerging trends and technologies shaping the e-commerce marketing landscape. From artificial intelligence and chatbots to voice search and virtual reality, we will discuss how businesses can leverage these innovations to stay ahead of the competition and provide exceptional customer experiences.

Whether you are an aspiring entrepreneur, a small business owner, or a digital marketing professional, this subchapter will equip you with the knowledge and tools necessary to excel in e-commerce marketing. By understanding the core principles and strategies outlined here, you can boost your online presence, drive results, and achieve success in the dynamic and ever-evolving digital business niche.

Setting up an Online Store

In this digital age, setting up an online store has become a crucial step for businesses to establish their presence and drive results in the competitive world of digital business. Whether you are an entrepreneur starting a new venture or an established brick-and-mortar store looking to expand your reach, creating an online store opens up a world of opportunities.

Before diving into the process, it is essential to understand the benefits of having an online store. Firstly, it allows you to tap into a global market, reaching customers beyond geographical boundaries. Additionally, an online store operates 24/7, ensuring that your products or services are available to customers at any time. This flexibility enhances customer convenience and increases the likelihood of making sales.

To set up an online store, there are several key steps you need to follow. The first step involves selecting the right platform for your store. There are numerous e-commerce platforms available, each with its own set of features and pricing structures. Researching and selecting the platform that aligns with your business needs is crucial.

Once you have chosen a platform, the next step is to design and customize your store. This involves selecting a visually appealing theme, creating a user-friendly interface, and integrating payment gateways to facilitate secure transactions. It is important to ensure that your online store reflects your brand identity and provides a seamless shopping experience for your customers.

After setting up the store, the next critical step is to optimize it for search engines. This involves implementing search engine optimization (SEO) techniques to improve your store's visibility on search engine result pages. By using relevant keywords, creating high-quality content, and optimizing product descriptions, you can attract organic traffic and increase your chances of making sales.

Furthermore, promoting your online store through various digital marketing channels is essential for success. Utilize social media platforms, email marketing, and paid advertising to drive traffic to your store and engage with your target audience. Building a strong online presence through consistent and targeted marketing efforts is key to achieving sustainable growth.

In conclusion, setting up an online store is a vital component of any digital business strategy. It enables you to expand your reach, increase convenience for customers, and maximize sales potential. By following the steps outlined above and employing effective digital marketing techniques, you can establish a successful online store that drives results and boosts your overall online presence.

E-commerce SEO and SEM Strategies

In today's digital age, having a strong online presence is vital for any business, especially for those operating in the digital business niche. E-commerce, in particular, requires a comprehensive understanding of search engine optimization (SEO) and search engine marketing (SEM) strategies to thrive in the highly competitive online marketplace. This subchapter will delve into the essential tactics and techniques that can help businesses boost their online visibility and drive results.

SEO, the backbone of any successful digital marketing strategy, plays a crucial role in improving a website's organic search rankings. It involves optimizing various on-page and off-page elements to make the website more search engine-friendly. From keyword research and optimization to creating high-quality content and building authoritative backlinks, every aspect of SEO contributes to higher visibility and increased organic traffic. The subchapter will explore these techniques and provide step-by-step guidance on implementing them effectively.

On the other hand, SEM focuses on utilizing paid advertising to drive targeted traffic to a website. It includes techniques such as pay-per-click (PPC) advertising, display ads, and remarketing campaigns. With SEM, businesses can quickly reach their target audience and generate instant results. The subchapter will explain the different SEM strategies, their benefits, and how to optimize campaigns for maximum return on investment.

Moreover, the subchapter will highlight the importance of integrating SEO and SEM strategies to create a comprehensive digital marketing approach. By combining both techniques, businesses can achieve a higher level of visibility and maximize their online presence. It will also provide insights into the latest industry trends, tools, and best practices to stay ahead in the ever-evolving world of e-commerce.

Whether you are a seasoned digital marketer or new to the digital business niche, this subchapter will serve as your ultimate guide to mastering SEO and SEM strategies for e-commerce success. By implementing the strategies outlined in this subchapter, you will be able to enhance your online visibility, increase traffic to your e-commerce website, and ultimately drive better results, including higher conversion rates and increased revenue.

In conclusion, understanding and implementing effective SEO and SEM strategies are essential for any e-commerce business looking to thrive in the digital marketplace. This subchapter will equip you with the knowledge and tools you need to boost your online presence and drive significant results in the highly competitive world of digital business.

Social Media Marketing for E-commerce

In today's digital age, social media has become an integral part of our lives. It has revolutionized the way we connect, communicate, and consume information. It comes as no surprise that social media has also transformed the way businesses operate, especially in the realm of e-commerce. This subchapter delves into the world of social media marketing for e-commerce, exploring the strategies and tactics that can help businesses thrive in the digital landscape.

Social media marketing offers a myriad of opportunities for e-commerce businesses to boost their online presence and drive tangible results. With platforms like Facebook, Instagram, Twitter, and LinkedIn, businesses can reach a wide audience, engage with potential customers, and build lasting relationships. However, to succeed in this competitive digital landscape, it is crucial to develop a comprehensive social media marketing strategy tailored to your e-commerce niche.

First and foremost, it is essential to identify your target audience and understand their preferences and behaviors on social media. This knowledge will help you create content that resonates with them, increasing the chances of conversions and sales. Furthermore, leveraging social media analytics tools can provide valuable insights into the performance of your campaigns, allowing you to make data-driven decisions and optimize your marketing efforts.

One of the key aspects of social media marketing for e-commerce is creating compelling and visually appealing content. High-quality images and videos showcasing your products or services can capture the attention of your audience and drive engagement. Additionally, user-generated content, such as customer reviews and testimonials, can enhance credibility and encourage potential customers to make a purchase.

Social media platforms also offer various advertising options to promote your e-commerce business. Facebook Ads, Instagram Ads, and Twitter Ads enable businesses to target specific demographics, interests, and behaviors, ensuring your message reaches the right people at the right time. Moreover, influencer marketing has emerged as a powerful tool in social media marketing, allowing e-commerce businesses to collaborate with influencers who have a significant following in their niche.

Finally, it is important to foster a strong community on social media by actively engaging with your audience. Responding to comments, messages, and reviews in a timely and personalized manner shows that you value your customers and their feedback. Additionally, running social media contests, offering exclusive promotions, and providing educational content can help build brand loyalty and keep your audience engaged.

In conclusion, social media marketing for e-commerce is a crucial component in building a successful digital business. By understanding your target audience, creating compelling content, leveraging advertising options, and fostering a strong community, you can boost your online presence, drive results, and stay ahead in the competitive digital landscape.

Retention Strategies for E-commerce

In the fast-paced world of digital business, e-commerce has become the go-to platform for entrepreneurs to showcase their products and services. However, with the increasing competition in the online marketplace, it has become crucial for businesses to implement effective retention strategies to keep customers coming back for more. In this subchapter, we will explore some tried-and-tested techniques that can help you boost customer loyalty and drive long-term success in your e-commerce venture.

1. Personalization: One of the key aspects of retaining customers in the digital business landscape is providing a personalized experience. Utilize data analytics and customer segmentation to understand your audience and their preferences better. Tailor your marketing messages, product recommendations, and offers to match their individual needs, creating a sense of exclusivity and connection.

2. Loyalty Programs: Implementing a robust loyalty program can significantly impact customer retention. Reward your customers for their repeat purchases or referrals with exclusive discounts, freebies, or early access to new products. This not only encourages them to keep coming back but also helps to foster a sense of belonging and appreciation.

3. Email Marketing: Email remains a powerful tool for engaging with customers and nurturing long-term relationships. Create a well-designed and informative newsletter that provides valuable content, exclusive offers, and personalized recommendations. Use triggered

emails to send abandoned cart reminders or follow-ups after a purchase to keep your brand top-of-mind.

4. Exceptional Customer Service: In the digital business world, customer service is often a make-or-break factor. Respond promptly to customer inquiries, address their concerns, and go the extra mile to provide exceptional support. Positive experiences with your brand will not only lead to repeat purchases but also generate positive word-of-mouth referrals.

5. User-generated Content: Leverage user-generated content to build trust and loyalty. Encourage customers to share their experiences, reviews, and testimonials on social media or your website. This not only helps to showcase your products but also creates a sense of community and authenticity around your brand.

6. Continuous Improvement: Stay ahead of the competition by continuously monitoring customer feedback, analyzing data, and making improvements to your e-commerce platform. Regularly update your website, optimize the user experience, and introduce new features to keep customers engaged and satisfied.

In conclusion, effective retention strategies are vital for sustained success in the digital business world. By personalizing the customer experience, implementing loyalty programs, leveraging email marketing, providing exceptional customer service, encouraging user-generated content, and continuously improving your e-commerce platform, you can build a loyal customer base and drive long-term growth.

Chapter 11: Marketing Automation

Introduction to Marketing Automation

In today's rapidly evolving digital landscape, marketing automation has become a crucial tool for businesses of all sizes. Whether you are an entrepreneur, a digital marketer, or a business owner, understanding the fundamentals of marketing automation is essential for driving results and boosting your online presence.

Marketing automation refers to the use of technology to automate repetitive marketing tasks and streamline marketing efforts. It allows businesses to engage with their audience in a personalized and efficient manner, leading to improved customer experiences and increased conversions.

This subchapter aims to provide a comprehensive introduction to marketing automation, covering its benefits, key components, and how it can be leveraged effectively in the digital business realm.

Benefits of Marketing Automation:
1. Time and Cost Efficiency: By automating repetitive tasks such as email marketing, lead nurturing, and social media posting, marketing automation saves valuable time and resources, allowing businesses to focus on other critical areas.
2. Personalized Customer Experiences: With advanced segmentation and targeting capabilities, marketing automation enables businesses to deliver personalized content and offers to their audience, enhancing customer satisfaction and loyalty.
3. Lead Generation and Nurturing: Marketing automation helps

identify and nurture leads throughout the customer journey, from initial awareness to the final purchase, increasing the chances of conversion.

4. Data-Driven Decision Making: By providing detailed analytics and insights, marketing automation empowers businesses to make data-driven decisions, optimize campaigns, and improve overall marketing effectiveness.

Key Components of Marketing Automation:

1. Customer Relationship Management (CRM): A CRM system forms the foundation of marketing automation, allowing businesses to manage customer data, track interactions, and segment audiences.

2. Email Marketing Automation: Automated email campaigns help nurture leads, engage with customers, and deliver personalized content based on user behavior and preferences.

3. Lead Scoring and Nurturing: Marketing automation platforms enable businesses to score leads based on their interactions, prioritize high-value prospects, and nurture them through targeted campaigns.

4. Social Media Automation: Automating social media posting, scheduling, and monitoring helps maintain an active online presence, engage with followers, and drive traffic to your website.

5. Analytics and Reporting: Marketing automation provides robust analytics and reporting features that allow businesses to measure the effectiveness of their campaigns, track ROI, and identify areas for improvement.

In this subchapter, we will delve into each of these components, exploring their functionalities, best practices, and how they can be integrated to create a comprehensive marketing automation strategy.

Whether you are a digital business owner, a marketer, or simply interested in understanding the world of marketing automation, this subchapter will equip you with the knowledge and tools to leverage this powerful technology, boost your online presence, and drive tangible results for your business.

Implementing Marketing Automation Tools

In today's fast-paced digital business landscape, marketing automation has become a crucial element for success. To stay competitive and drive results, businesses must harness the power of technology to streamline their marketing efforts. This subchapter will delve into the concept of implementing marketing automation tools and how they can revolutionize your online presence.

Marketing automation involves using software platforms to automate repetitive marketing tasks, such as email campaigns, social media posting, lead nurturing, and customer segmentation. By utilizing these tools effectively, businesses can save time, improve efficiency, and deliver personalized experiences to their target audience.

One of the primary benefits of marketing automation is its ability to nurture leads and guide them through the sales funnel. By implementing automated email campaigns, businesses can deliver timely and relevant content to prospects, increasing the chances of conversion. Additionally, marketing automation tools can track user behavior and engagement, allowing businesses to analyze data and make informed decisions about their marketing strategies.

Another advantage of marketing automation is its impact on customer engagement. By segmenting customers based on their preferences, demographics, or past interactions, businesses can tailor their marketing messages to specific groups. This personalization enhances the overall customer experience, leading to increased brand loyalty and retention.

Furthermore, marketing automation tools can help businesses optimize their social media presence. By scheduling posts in advance, monitoring engagement metrics, and analyzing the performance of different campaigns, businesses can fine-tune their social media strategies for maximum impact. This enables them to reach a wider audience, build brand awareness, and engage with potential customers more efficiently.

When implementing marketing automation tools, it is crucial to choose the right platform that aligns with your business goals and objectives. Conduct thorough research, read reviews, and consider the scalability and integrations of the software. Moreover, it is essential to invest time in training your team to fully utilize the tools' capabilities and maximize their benefits.

In conclusion, marketing automation tools have become indispensable for digital businesses looking to boost their online presence and drive results. By automating repetitive tasks, nurturing leads efficiently, personalizing customer experiences, and optimizing social media strategies, businesses can achieve higher conversion rates, increased customer engagement, and improved overall marketing performance. Implementing marketing automation tools is not only a wise business decision but also a necessary step in the ever-evolving digital marketing landscape.

Lead Generation and Nurturing with Marketing Automation

In the ever-evolving world of digital business, lead generation and nurturing have become critical components of any successful marketing strategy. The ability to attract potential customers and nurture them through the sales funnel is essential for driving growth and achieving business objectives. This is where marketing automation comes into play, offering a powerful toolset to streamline and optimize lead generation efforts.

Marketing automation refers to the use of technology to automate repetitive marketing tasks and workflows, allowing businesses to reach their target audience more effectively and efficiently. It enables marketers to automate lead capture, nurturing, and qualification processes, resulting in improved lead quality and higher conversion rates.

One of the primary benefits of marketing automation is its ability to generate leads. By leveraging various digital channels, such as social media, email marketing, and content marketing, businesses can capture valuable information from potential customers. Marketing automation software can then automatically segment and categorize these leads based on predefined criteria, ensuring that the right message is delivered to the right audience at the right time.

Once leads are captured, nurturing them becomes crucial. Marketing automation allows businesses to create personalized and targeted campaigns to engage and educate leads throughout their buying journey. By delivering relevant content, such as blog posts, whitepapers, or webinars, businesses can build trust and credibility with their prospects, increasing the likelihood of conversion.

Moreover, marketing automation enables businesses to track and analyze the behavior of their leads, providing valuable insights into their interests, preferences, and readiness to purchase. With this information, marketers can develop highly targeted and personalized campaigns, tailored to the specific needs and pain points of each lead.

Furthermore, marketing automation allows for the automation of repetitive tasks, such as scheduling emails, sending follow-ups, and managing lead scoring. This not only saves time and resources but also ensures consistent and timely communication with leads, enhancing the overall customer experience.

In conclusion, lead generation and nurturing are essential for success in the digital business landscape. The use of marketing automation tools can significantly enhance these efforts by automating lead capture, nurturing, and qualification processes. By leveraging the power of technology, businesses can attract, engage, and convert leads more effectively, ultimately driving results and boosting their online presence.

Personalization and Segmentation in Marketing Automation

In today's fast-paced digital business landscape, personalization and segmentation have become crucial strategies for marketers to boost their online presence and drive results. With the ever-increasing amount of data available, businesses can now tailor their marketing efforts to reach their target audiences more effectively.

Personalization involves creating customized experiences for individual customers based on their preferences, behaviors, and demographics. It goes beyond simply addressing customers by their names; it's about understanding their needs and delivering relevant content at the right time. By personalizing their marketing campaigns, businesses can establish deeper connections with their customers and enhance their overall experience.

On the other hand, segmentation involves dividing a larger target audience into smaller, more specific groups based on factors like age, location, interests, and purchase history. By segmenting their audience, businesses can create highly targeted marketing campaigns that resonate with each group's unique characteristics and preferences. This approach allows marketers to deliver more relevant and compelling offers, increasing the chances of conversion.

Marketing automation plays a vital role in implementing personalization and segmentation strategies at scale. By leveraging advanced software and tools, businesses can automate repetitive marketing tasks and deliver personalized content to thousands of customers simultaneously. Automation also enables marketers to track and analyze customer behavior, allowing them to refine their strategies and improve their campaign performance over time.

By combining personalization and segmentation with marketing automation, businesses can achieve significant benefits. Firstly, personalized and segmented campaigns have higher engagement rates and conversion rates compared to generic mass marketing. Customers are more likely to respond positively to messages that resonate with their specific needs and interests.

Secondly, personalization and segmentation help businesses build stronger customer relationships and foster brand loyalty. When customers feel valued and understood, they are more likely to remain loyal and become advocates for the brand. This, in turn, leads to increased customer retention and higher customer lifetime value.

Lastly, personalization and segmentation allow businesses to optimize their marketing budget by targeting only the most relevant audience segments. By focusing on the right customers, businesses can maximize their return on investment and allocate resources more efficiently.

In conclusion, personalization and segmentation are essential strategies in the digital marketing landscape. By leveraging marketing automation tools, businesses can deliver personalized experiences to their target audience at scale, resulting in higher engagement, stronger customer relationships, and improved ROI. As the digital business environment continues to evolve, mastering these techniques will be crucial for any marketer looking to succeed in the online realm.

Analyzing and Optimizing Marketing Automation Campaigns

In today's fast-paced digital business landscape, marketing automation has become a critical tool for businesses of all sizes to streamline their marketing efforts and drive results. However, simply setting up a marketing automation campaign is not enough. To truly harness the power of automation and maximize its potential, it is essential to analyze and optimize your campaigns.

Analyzing your marketing automation campaigns allows you to gain valuable insights into the effectiveness of your strategies and identify areas for improvement. By closely monitoring key performance indicators (KPIs) such as open rates, click-through rates, conversion rates, and customer engagement, you can measure the success of your campaigns and make data-driven decisions.

One crucial aspect of analyzing marketing automation campaigns is tracking customer behavior and engagement. By understanding how your audience interacts with your emails, landing pages, and other marketing assets, you can tailor your campaigns to deliver personalized and relevant content. This will not only improve customer satisfaction but also increase the chances of conversions and sales.

Another vital aspect of optimizing marketing automation campaigns is A/B testing. By testing different variations of your emails, subject lines, CTAs, and landing pages, you can identify which elements resonate best with your target audience. This iterative testing process allows you to continuously refine and enhance your campaigns, ensuring that you are delivering the most impactful messages to your customers.

Furthermore, segmenting your audience is a crucial optimization strategy. By dividing your customer base into smaller, more targeted groups based on demographics, behavior, or interests, you can create highly personalized campaigns that resonate with each segment. This level of personalization significantly increases the chances of conversions and fosters stronger customer relationships.

In addition to analyzing and optimizing individual marketing automation campaigns, it is essential to take a holistic approach to your digital marketing strategy. By integrating your marketing automation efforts with other digital channels such as social media, content marketing, and SEO, you can create a seamless and cohesive customer journey. This cross-channel integration ensures that your messaging is consistent, and your marketing efforts work together to achieve your business goals.

In conclusion, analyzing and optimizing marketing automation campaigns is a crucial step in maximizing the effectiveness of your digital business. By closely monitoring key metrics, testing different variations, segmenting your audience, and integrating your efforts across channels, you can drive better results and enhance your online presence. Stay tuned for the next chapter, where we will dive deeper into the various tools and techniques available to help you succeed in your digital marketing endeavors.

Chapter 12: Emerging Trends in Digital Marketing

Artificial Intelligence (AI) in Digital Marketing

In today's rapidly evolving digital business landscape, staying ahead of the competition is essential to drive results and boost your online presence. One of the most powerful tools available to digital marketers is Artificial Intelligence (AI). AI has revolutionized the way businesses interact with their customers, analyze data, and optimize marketing strategies. In this subchapter, we will explore the various applications of AI in digital marketing and how it can benefit everyone involved in the digital business niche.

AI in digital marketing encompasses a wide range of technologies and techniques that enable businesses to automate tasks, streamline processes, and deliver personalized experiences to their target audience. One of the key areas where AI excels is data analysis. With the ability to process vast amounts of data quickly and accurately, AI algorithms can uncover valuable insights that would take humans weeks or even months to discover. By analyzing customer behavior, preferences, and purchase patterns, businesses can tailor their marketing campaigns to target specific segments effectively.

AI-powered chatbots are another popular application of AI in digital marketing. These virtual assistants can engage with customers in real-time, answering their queries and providing personalized recommendations. AI chatbots are available 24/7, ensuring that businesses never miss an opportunity to connect with their audience. Moreover, these chatbots can learn from every interaction, continuously improving their responses and understanding of customer needs.

Personalization is a key aspect of successful digital marketing, and AI plays a crucial role in delivering tailored experiences. By leveraging AI algorithms, businesses can analyze customer data to create personalized content, product recommendations, and targeted advertisements. This level of personalization not only enhances the customer experience but also increases conversion rates and customer loyalty.

Furthermore, AI can optimize digital marketing campaigns by automating various tasks such as A/B testing, ad placement, and content creation. AI algorithms can analyze campaign performance in real-time, making data-driven decisions to maximize return on investment. By automating these repetitive tasks, businesses can save time and resources, allowing them to focus on more strategic initiatives.

In conclusion, AI is transforming the digital marketing landscape, providing businesses in the digital business niche with powerful tools to boost their online presence and drive results. By harnessing the capabilities of AI, businesses can analyze data, personalize experiences, and optimize marketing campaigns like never before. Whether you are a marketer, entrepreneur, or digital business owner, understanding and embracing AI in digital marketing is crucial to stay competitive in today's dynamic digital world.

Voice Search and Digital Assistants

In today's fast-paced digital era, voice search and digital assistants have emerged as game-changers in the world of digital business. With the advent of smart speakers, virtual assistants like Siri, Alexa, and Google Assistant, and the widespread use of smartphones, voice search has become an integral part of our daily lives. This subchapter aims to delve into the significance of voice search and digital assistants in the realm of digital marketing, catering to a diverse audience interested in enhancing their online presence and driving tangible results.

Voice search technology has revolutionized the way people interact with the internet. Instead of typing in search queries, users can now simply ask questions or make requests verbally, and the digital assistants provide instant answers or perform desired actions. This seamless user experience has led to a significant rise in voice search queries, making it crucial for businesses to optimize their digital presence accordingly.

One of the key advantages of voice search is its convenience. People can perform searches while driving, cooking, or simply multitasking, enabling them to access information effortlessly. As a result, businesses need to adapt their digital marketing strategies to cater to this growing trend. Optimizing website content for voice search, using long-tail keywords, and providing concise and direct answers via featured snippets are some effective techniques to stay ahead in this competitive landscape.

Digital assistants also open up new avenues for businesses to engage with their customers. Brands can develop voice-activated applications, also known as skills or actions, to provide personalized and interactive experiences. For example, a clothing retailer could create an Alexa skill that allows users to ask for fashion advice or style recommendations based on their preferences. By leveraging digital assistants, businesses can enhance customer engagement, build brand loyalty, and gain a competitive edge.

Furthermore, voice search and digital assistants have significant implications for local businesses. With the increasing use of voice search for local queries such as "near me" searches, it is crucial for businesses to optimize their online listings and ensure accurate and up-to-date information is readily available. This includes optimizing for local SEO, leveraging customer reviews, and ensuring accurate business information across various platforms.

In conclusion, voice search and digital assistants have revolutionized the digital business landscape, presenting both challenges and opportunities for marketers. By adapting their digital marketing strategies to accommodate voice search, businesses can boost their online presence, engage with customers on a more personal level, and achieve tangible results. Embracing this technology-driven trend is essential for any individual or business seeking to thrive in the ever-evolving world of digital marketing.

Augmented Reality (AR) and Virtual Reality (VR)

In the ever-evolving landscape of digital business, technology continues to push the boundaries of what is possible. Two technological advancements that have gained significant traction in recent years are Augmented Reality (AR) and Virtual Reality (VR). These immersive experiences have revolutionized the way businesses engage with their customers and offer endless possibilities for enhancing online presence.

Augmented Reality (AR) is the integration of digital information into the real world, creating an interactive experience that blurs the lines between the physical and digital realms. With the use of smartphones, tablets, or specialized AR glasses, users can overlay computer-generated images onto their surroundings. This technology has been widely adopted by various industries, from retail and e-commerce to gaming and entertainment.

By incorporating AR into their digital strategies, businesses can offer customers a unique and interactive shopping experience. For example, furniture retailers can allow customers to visualize how a particular piece of furniture would look in their homes before making a purchase. This not only enhances customer satisfaction but also reduces the likelihood of returns, ultimately boosting the bottom line.

On the other hand, Virtual Reality (VR) creates a completely immersive, computer-generated environment. Users can step into a virtual world through specialized headsets, completely disconnecting from the physical surroundings. While VR initially gained popularity in the gaming industry, its potential has expanded to other sectors as well.

For businesses, VR offers a powerful tool for storytelling and brand engagement. Companies can create virtual experiences that transport customers to different locations, showcase products in a captivating way, or provide virtual tours of real estate properties. These immersive experiences leave a lasting impression on customers and enhance brand recognition.

Both AR and VR hold immense potential for digital marketers. By embracing these technologies, businesses can differentiate themselves from competitors and offer unique experiences to their customers. However, it is crucial to carefully consider the target audience and the goals of the marketing campaign before implementing AR or VR.

In conclusion, Augmented Reality (AR) and Virtual Reality (VR) have transformed the way businesses connect with customers in the digital world. Whether it's overlaying digital information onto the real world or creating immersive virtual environments, these technologies offer endless opportunities for enhancing online presence and driving results. By leveraging AR and VR, businesses can captivate their audience, increase customer engagement, and ultimately boost their digital business.

Chatbots and Conversational Marketing

In today's fast-paced digital business landscape, staying ahead of the competition requires innovative and efficient strategies. One such strategy that has gained immense popularity is the use of chatbots for conversational marketing. Chatbots have revolutionized the way businesses interact with their customers, offering personalized and seamless experiences that drive results.

But what exactly are chatbots? Simply put, chatbots are computer programs designed to simulate human conversation and provide instant responses to customer queries. These intelligent virtual assistants are programmed to understand and interpret natural language, allowing businesses to engage with their audience in real-time.

The rise of chatbots in digital marketing can be attributed to their ability to automate and streamline customer interactions. Instead of waiting for a human representative to respond, chatbots provide instant support, enhancing customer satisfaction and reducing response times. This efficiency not only improves the overall customer experience but also frees up valuable time for businesses to focus on other important tasks.

Conversational marketing, on the other hand, refers to the practice of engaging customers in two-way conversations to build stronger relationships and drive conversions. By leveraging chatbots, businesses can create personalized experiences that cater to individual customer needs. Through interactive conversations, chatbots can gather relevant customer information and provide tailored recommendations, ultimately increasing customer engagement and loyalty.

One of the key advantages of chatbots in conversational marketing is their availability 24/7. Unlike traditional customer service channels that have limited operating hours, chatbots are always ready to assist customers at any time of the day. This round-the-clock availability ensures that businesses never miss out on potential leads or sales opportunities, regardless of the time zone or location.

Moreover, chatbots can be integrated with various digital platforms, including websites, social media, and messaging apps, allowing businesses to reach customers wherever they are. This omnichannel approach ensures a consistent and seamless customer experience across different touchpoints, further enhancing brand reputation and customer satisfaction.

In conclusion, chatbots and conversational marketing have revolutionized the way businesses interact with their customers in the digital realm. By leveraging the efficiency and personalization offered by chatbots, businesses can enhance customer experiences, drive conversions, and stay ahead in the competitive digital landscape. So, whether you are a small startup or a large corporation, incorporating chatbots into your digital marketing strategy is crucial to boost your online presence and drive tangible results.

Blockchain Technology and Cryptocurrency in Marketing

In this rapidly evolving digital landscape, it is crucial for businesses to keep up with the latest trends and technologies in order to stay ahead of the competition. One such technology that has been making waves in recent years is blockchain, and its associated digital currency, cryptocurrency. In this subchapter, we will explore the potential applications of blockchain technology and cryptocurrency in the field of marketing, and how they can revolutionize the way businesses connect with their target audience.

Blockchain technology, at its core, is a decentralized and transparent ledger system that securely records transactions across multiple computers. This technology has the potential to bring about significant changes in the marketing industry by increasing transparency, reducing fraud, and improving customer trust. For example, blockchain can be used to create tamper-proof digital identities for customers, ensuring that their personal information remains secure and protected. This not only enhances customer privacy but also helps businesses build trust and credibility with their target audience.

Furthermore, cryptocurrency, which is powered by blockchain technology, can also play a significant role in marketing. By accepting cryptocurrencies as a form of payment, businesses can open up new revenue streams and tap into a global market. Cryptocurrencies eliminate the need for intermediaries such as banks, thus reducing transaction costs and increasing efficiency. This can be particularly beneficial for businesses operating in the digital realm, as it enables them to conduct transactions quickly and securely across borders.

Additionally, blockchain technology can transform the way businesses conduct marketing campaigns. Its decentralized nature allows for the creation of smart contracts, which are self-executing contracts with the terms of the agreement directly written into code. These smart contracts can automate various marketing processes, such as tracking customer engagement, managing loyalty programs, and distributing rewards. This not only streamlines operations but also provides businesses with valuable insights into customer behavior, enabling them to tailor their marketing strategies more effectively.

While blockchain technology and cryptocurrency hold immense potential, it is essential for businesses to approach their adoption with caution. As with any emerging technology, there are risks and challenges that need to be considered. Therefore, it is crucial for businesses to conduct thorough research, seek expert advice, and stay updated with the latest developments in this field.

In conclusion, blockchain technology and cryptocurrency have the potential to revolutionize the marketing industry. By leveraging the transparency, security, and efficiency that these technologies offer, businesses can enhance customer trust, streamline operations, and tap into new markets. However, it is important for businesses to approach their adoption with careful consideration and always stay informed about the latest advancements in this rapidly evolving field.

Chapter 13: Building a Successful Digital Marketing Career

Essential Skills for a Digital Marketer

In today's digital age, having a strong online presence is crucial for businesses of all sizes. Whether you are a seasoned entrepreneur or just starting out in the digital business world, understanding the essential skills required to succeed as a digital marketer is paramount. This subchapter aims to equip you with the knowledge and tools necessary to navigate the ever-evolving landscape of digital marketing and drive results for your online ventures.

1. Data Analysis: In the realm of digital marketing, data is king. Being able to analyze and interpret data is essential for making informed decisions and optimizing your online campaigns. Familiarize yourself with tools like Google Analytics and learn how to extract meaningful insights to improve your marketing strategies.

2. Content Creation: Engaging and high-quality content is at the core of any successful digital marketing campaign. Develop your skills in content creation, including writing, graphic design, videography, and photography. Understand the importance of storytelling and how to create content that resonates with your target audience.

3. SEO and SEM: Search Engine Optimization (SEO) and Search Engine Marketing (SEM) are crucial for driving organic and paid traffic to your website. Learn about keyword research, on-page optimization, link building, and the effective use of pay-per-click advertising to enhance your online visibility.

4. Social Media Marketing: Social media platforms have become powerful marketing tools. Understand how to leverage platforms like Facebook, Instagram, Twitter, and LinkedIn to reach and engage with your target audience. Learn about content planning, community management, and advertising on social media.

5. Email Marketing: Despite the rise of other digital communication channels, email marketing remains one of the most effective ways to nurture leads and drive conversions. Learn how to build and segment email lists, create compelling email content, and measure the success of your email campaigns.

6. Conversion Rate Optimization: A successful digital marketer knows how to optimize websites and landing pages to maximize conversion rates. Learn about A/B testing, user experience (UX) design, and website analytics to improve the overall performance of your online assets.

7. Digital Advertising: Gain expertise in digital advertising platforms such as Google Ads, Facebook Ads, and display advertising networks. Understand how to effectively target your audience, create compelling ad copy, and measure the return on investment (ROI) of your advertising campaigns.

8. Continuous Learning: The digital marketing landscape is constantly evolving, so it is crucial to stay updated with the latest trends and best practices. Engage in continuous learning by attending webinars, conferences, and online courses, and join relevant industry communities to stay ahead of the curve.

By developing these essential skills, you will be well-equipped to boost your online presence, drive results, and succeed in the dynamic world of digital business. Remember, digital marketing is a journey, and continuous improvement and adaptation are key to achieving long-term success.

Navigating the Job Market in Digital Marketing

In today's fast-paced digital business landscape, having a strong online presence is crucial for success. As more businesses recognize the importance of digital marketing, the job market in this field has become increasingly competitive. However, with the right strategies and skills, you can stand out and thrive in the digital marketing job market.

One of the first steps in navigating the job market is to understand the various roles and positions available in digital marketing. From social media management to search engine optimization, content creation to email marketing, there are numerous career paths to explore. By identifying your interests and strengths, you can choose a niche that aligns with your passion and skills.

Once you have identified your niche, it is important to acquire the necessary skills and knowledge. Digital marketing is an ever-evolving field, and staying updated with the latest trends and technologies is essential. Enrolling in relevant courses, attending webinars, and joining industry-specific communities can help you stay ahead of the curve.

Building a strong online presence is also crucial in today's digital age. Employers often look for candidates who can demonstrate their expertise through a personal website, blog, or active social media profiles. By showcasing your knowledge and skills in the digital marketing field, you can attract potential employers and stand out from the competition.

Networking plays a significant role in finding job opportunities in digital marketing. Attend industry conferences, join professional groups, and connect with like-minded individuals on platforms such as LinkedIn. Engaging in conversations, sharing insights, and building relationships can open doors to potential job opportunities and collaborations.

When applying for digital marketing positions, it is important to tailor your resume and cover letter to highlight relevant skills and experiences. Emphasize your proficiency in various digital marketing tools, your understanding of data analytics, and any successful campaigns you have been a part of. Additionally, showcasing your ability to adapt to new technologies and trends can give you an edge in this competitive job market.

Finally, during interviews, be prepared to discuss your digital marketing strategies, explain how you have achieved results in the past, and showcase your problem-solving skills. Employers often value candidates who can think critically, adapt quickly, and show a genuine passion for the field.

Navigating the job market in digital marketing may seem daunting, but with the right mindset, skills, and strategies, you can find success. By continuously learning, building your online presence, networking, and showcasing your expertise, you can position yourself as a sought-after professional in the digital marketing field.

Building a Personal Brand in the Digital Marketing Industry

In today's hyper-connected world, building a personal brand is crucial, especially in the fast-paced and ever-evolving digital marketing industry. Whether you are a seasoned professional or just starting your journey in the digital business realm, developing a strong personal brand can significantly boost your online presence and drive results.

First and foremost, it is important to understand what a personal brand entails. Your personal brand is the image and reputation you cultivate for yourself in the digital marketing industry. It encompasses your skills, expertise, values, and unique perspective. It is the way others perceive and recognize you in the online world.

To build a powerful personal brand, start by defining your niche and expertise within the digital marketing industry. Identify your strengths and passions. Are you an expert in social media marketing, content creation, SEO, or email marketing? Focusing on a specific area of expertise will help you stand out and position yourself as an authority in that field.

Once you have identified your niche, it's time to showcase your knowledge and skills. Leverage various online platforms to establish your online presence. Create a professional website or blog where you can share valuable insights and tips related to digital marketing. Consistently produce high-quality content that resonates with your target audience. This will not only demonstrate your expertise but also help you build credibility and trust.

Additionally, actively participate in relevant online communities and engage with industry influencers. Join digital marketing forums,

LinkedIn groups, and Facebook communities where you can contribute to discussions and share your insights. Collaborate with other like-minded professionals and seek opportunities to guest post on reputable industry websites or publications. This will expand your reach and expose you to a wider audience.

Building a personal brand also involves nurturing and maintaining relationships with your audience. Respond to comments, messages, and inquiries promptly. Cultivate a genuine and authentic online persona that reflects your values and expertise. Consistency and transparency are key in establishing trust and loyalty among your followers.

Lastly, never stop learning and growing. The digital marketing industry is constantly evolving, and staying up-to-date with the latest trends and technologies is essential. Attend industry conferences, webinars, and workshops. Read books and blogs written by industry thought leaders. Continuously refine your skills and adapt to the changing landscape of digital marketing.

By building a personal brand in the digital marketing industry, you will not only position yourself as an expert but also open doors to new opportunities, collaborations, and career growth. So, take the time to invest in developing your personal brand and watch as it propels you towards success in the dynamic world of digital business.

Continuing Education and Professional Development

In the rapidly evolving landscape of digital business, it is crucial for professionals to constantly update their knowledge and skills to stay ahead of the game. This is where continuing education and professional development come into play. In this subchapter, we will explore the importance of ongoing learning and provide valuable insights on how to boost your online presence and drive results in the ever-changing world of digital marketing.

Continuing education is not just a luxury; it is a necessity for anyone involved in the digital business industry. With technology advancing at an unprecedented pace, digital marketers need to stay updated on the latest trends, tools, and strategies to remain competitive. Whether you are a newcomer in the field or a seasoned professional, investing in your professional development is key to sustaining success.

One of the primary benefits of continuing education is the opportunity to expand your knowledge base. By attending workshops, seminars, webinars, or online courses, you can gain insights from industry experts and thought leaders. This exposure to new ideas and perspectives can fuel innovation and enhance your problem-solving skills, enabling you to tackle the challenges of the digital world with confidence.

Moreover, continuous learning allows you to adapt to emerging technologies and changing consumer behaviors. As the digital landscape evolves, so do the preferences and expectations of online users. By staying informed about the latest trends and techniques, you can optimize your online presence and deliver exceptional customer experiences.

Professional development also plays a crucial role in career advancement. By acquiring new skills and certifications, you can demonstrate your commitment to excellence and differentiate yourself from the competition. Employers are increasingly seeking digital professionals with a growth mindset and a willingness to learn. By investing in your education, you enhance your marketability and open doors to exciting career opportunities.

To make the most of your continuing education and professional development journey, it is essential to have a growth mindset. Embrace a lifelong learning approach and seek out opportunities to expand your knowledge and skills. Stay curious, network with industry peers, and leverage the power of online communities and resources.

Remember, in the world of digital marketing, the only constant is change. Embrace the challenges and seize the opportunities by investing in your education and professional development. By doing so, you can boost your online presence, drive results, and achieve long-term success in the dynamic world of digital business.

Success Stories and Inspiration from Digital Marketing Experts

In today's rapidly evolving digital landscape, digital marketing has become a crucial component of any successful business strategy. As the world continues to shift towards a more technologically advanced society, it is imperative for businesses to adapt and thrive in the online realm. This subchapter highlights success stories and offers inspiration from digital marketing experts who have achieved remarkable results in the ever-changing digital business niche.

One such success story is the journey of Sarah Thompson, a young entrepreneur who transformed her small online boutique into a global fashion brand through strategic digital marketing efforts. By leveraging social media platforms, email marketing, and influencer collaborations, Sarah was able to connect with her target audience and create a strong online presence. Her story serves as a testament to the power of digital marketing in helping businesses expand their reach and achieve tangible results.

Another inspiring digital marketing expert is John Williams, a seasoned marketer who revolutionized the fitness industry through innovative online advertising techniques. By utilizing data-driven insights and optimizing his campaigns across various channels, John was able to drive significant traffic to his fitness app and attract a large user base. His story showcases the immense potential of digital marketing to disrupt traditional industries and create new opportunities for growth and success.

Furthermore, this subchapter explores the inspiring journey of Jane Adams, a digital marketing consultant who specializes in helping startups and small businesses establish a strong online presence. Through her expertise in search engine optimization (SEO) and content marketing, Jane has enabled numerous businesses to increase their organic visibility and drive targeted traffic to their websites. Her story highlights the importance of digital marketing for businesses of all sizes, emphasizing that even with limited resources, entrepreneurs can achieve remarkable results through strategic digital marketing efforts.

These success stories from digital marketing experts serve as a source of inspiration and motivation for anyone seeking to enhance their online presence and drive results. Whether you are a small business owner, a marketing professional, or an aspiring entrepreneur, the experiences and insights shared by these experts can provide valuable lessons and actionable strategies to boost your digital business. By learning from their triumphs and challenges, you can gain the knowledge and confidence to navigate the dynamic world of digital marketing and achieve your own success story.

Chapter 14: Conclusion

Recap of Key Concepts

In this subchapter, we will take a moment to recap the key concepts discussed throughout this book, "The Ultimate Guide to Digital Marketing: Boost Your Online Presence and Drive Results." Whether you are a seasoned digital marketer or just starting out in the world of digital business, this recap will serve as a valuable summary of the key ideas and strategies covered.

1. Digital Marketing Fundamentals: We began by establishing a strong foundation in digital marketing, covering essential concepts such as the customer journey, target audience segmentation, and the importance of setting clear goals and objectives.

2. Website Optimization: A well-optimized website is crucial for success in the digital business world. We discussed the importance of user experience (UX), responsive design, search engine optimization (SEO), and the role of compelling content in engaging visitors and driving conversions.

3. Social Media Marketing: Social media platforms have become indispensable tools for businesses to connect with their audience. We explored the various social media channels, the importance of creating a cohesive brand presence, and the strategies for driving engagement and building a loyal community.

4. Content Marketing: Content is king, and we delved into the world of content marketing, discussing the different types of content, the power

of storytelling, and the strategies for creating valuable and shareable content that resonates with your target audience.

5. Email Marketing: While often overlooked, email marketing remains one of the most effective digital marketing channels. We covered the essentials of crafting compelling email campaigns, building an engaged subscriber list, and personalizing email content for maximum impact.

6. Pay-Per-Click Advertising: Pay-per-click (PPC) advertising allows businesses to reach their target audience through targeted ads. We explored the process of setting up effective PPC campaigns, conducting keyword research, optimizing ad copy, and tracking campaign performance.

7. Analytics and Measurement: To ensure the success of your digital marketing efforts, it is crucial to track and measure your results. We discussed the various analytics tools available, the key metrics to monitor, and the process of analyzing data to make informed decisions and optimize your campaigns.

By revisiting these key concepts, you will have a solid grasp of the fundamental strategies and tactics needed to excel in the world of digital business. Whether you are looking to boost your online presence, drive conversions, or enhance customer engagement, this book provides you with the knowledge and tools necessary to achieve your goals. Keep this recap handy as a reference guide, and continue to adapt and refine your digital marketing strategies as the landscape evolves.

Final Thoughts and Actionable Steps

Congratulations! You have reached the final chapter of "The Ultimate Guide to Digital Marketing: Boost Your Online Presence and Drive Results." Throughout this book, we have explored the vast world of digital marketing and provided you with valuable insights and strategies to enhance your online presence. Now, it's time to reflect on what you have learned and take actionable steps to propel your digital business forward.

In today's digital age, having a strong online presence is crucial for any business. Whether you are a small startup or an established company, embracing digital marketing strategies is the key to staying competitive in the market. By adopting the right tactics, you can attract more customers, increase brand awareness, and ultimately drive better results.

As you embark on your digital marketing journey, keep in mind that success doesn't happen overnight. It requires consistent effort, dedication, and a willingness to adapt to the ever-changing digital landscape. To help you get started, here are some actionable steps you can take:

1. Define Your Goals: Before diving into any digital marketing activities, clearly define your goals. Whether it's increasing website traffic, generating leads, or improving conversion rates, setting specific and measurable objectives will guide your strategy.

2. Know Your Audience: Understanding your target audience is crucial for effective digital marketing. Conduct thorough market research to identify their needs, preferences, and pain points. Tailor

your content and messaging to resonate with your audience and address their unique challenges.

3. Develop a Strong Brand Identity: Your brand is what sets you apart from your competitors. Craft a compelling brand story, design a visually appealing logo, and maintain consistent branding across all digital platforms. This will help you build trust and establish a strong brand presence.

4. Utilize Social Media: Social media platforms provide an excellent opportunity to engage with your audience and promote your brand. Identify the platforms that your target audience frequents, create compelling content, and actively interact with your followers.

5. Optimize Your Website: Your website is the face of your business in the digital world. Ensure it is user-friendly, visually appealing, and optimized for search engines. Conduct regular audits to identify areas for improvement and implement necessary changes.

6. Measure and Analyze: Implement analytics tools to track the performance of your digital marketing campaigns. Analyze the data to gain insights into what works and what doesn't. Use this information to refine your strategies and optimize your results.

Remember, digital marketing is an ongoing process. Stay up to date with the latest trends, experiment with different strategies, and continuously refine your approach. By taking these actionable steps and remaining committed to your digital marketing efforts, you will boost your online presence, drive results, and ultimately achieve success in the digital business world.

So, go forth, embrace the power of digital marketing, and watch your business thrive in the ever-evolving digital landscape. Good luck!

Taking Your Digital Marketing Efforts to the Next Level

In today's digital age, having a strong online presence is crucial for the success of any business. Whether you're a small startup or a well-established company, digital marketing is the key to reaching your target audience and driving results. To truly thrive in the digital business world, it's important to take your digital marketing efforts to the next level.

One of the first steps in taking your digital marketing to new heights is understanding your audience. Every successful digital marketing strategy begins with a deep understanding of who your target audience is and what they want. By conducting thorough market research and analyzing data, you can gain valuable insights into your customers' preferences, behaviors, and needs. This knowledge will enable you to create personalized and compelling marketing campaigns that truly resonate with your audience.

Next, it's crucial to optimize your website for search engines. Search engine optimization (SEO) plays a vital role in driving organic traffic to your website. By implementing effective SEO techniques such as keyword research, on-page optimization, and link building, you can improve your website's visibility in search engine results. This will not only increase your chances of attracting more visitors, but also enhance your brand's credibility and authority.

In addition to SEO, leveraging social media platforms is another powerful way to take your digital marketing efforts to the next level. Social media marketing allows you to connect with your audience on a more personal level, build brand awareness, and drive engagement. By creating high-quality content tailored to each platform and utilizing social media analytics, you can optimize your social media presence and effectively reach your target audience.

Furthermore, exploring the world of influencer marketing can significantly boost your digital marketing efforts. Influencers have a strong following and can help you expand your reach and credibility. Collaborating with influencers who align with your brand values and have a relevant audience can lead to increased brand awareness and conversions.

Lastly, never underestimate the power of analytics and data-driven decision making. By regularly analyzing your digital marketing performance, you can identify what strategies are working and what needs improvement. This data-driven approach allows you to make informed decisions and continuously optimize your digital marketing efforts for better results.

In conclusion, taking your digital marketing efforts to the next level is essential for success in the digital business world. By understanding your audience, optimizing your website for search engines, leveraging social media, exploring influencer marketing, and using analytics to drive decision making, you can significantly boost your online presence and drive tangible results. Embrace the power of digital marketing and propel your business to new heights.

www.ingramcontent.com/pod-product-compliance
Lightning Source LLC
LaVergne TN
LVHW021828060526
838201LV00058B/3553